RAND NATIONAL DEFENSE RESEARCH INSTITUTE

The Center for Excellence in Disaster Management and Humanitarian Assistance (CFE-DMHA)

An Assessment of Roles and Missions

Stephanie Pezard, David E. Thaler, Beth Grill, Ariel Klein, Sean Robson

T0308358

Prepared for the Office of the Secretary of Defense for Policy

For more information on this publication, visit www.rand.org/t/rr1332

Library of Congress Cataloging-in-Publication Data
ISBN: 978-0-8330-9218-2

Published by the RAND Corporation, Santa Monica, Calif.
© Copyright 2016 RAND Corporation
RAND® is a registered trademark.

Support RAND
Make a tax-deductible charitable contribution at
www.rand.org/giving/contribute

www.rand.org

Preface

In recognition of the important role that the U.S. military has to play in humanitarian assistance and disaster relief, congressional legislation established the Center for Excellence in Disaster Management and Humanitarian Assistance (CFE-DMHA) in Honolulu in 1994 to provide and facilitate education, training, and research in civil-military operations in this field. This report examines CFE-DMHA's history and activities to help determine how the missions assigned to it can best be performed to meet the challenges facing the U.S. Department of Defense (DoD) in this domain. The report finds that a center focused on disaster management and humanitarian assistance (DMHA) fulfills important needs that will only grow in the future. After identifying some key concerns with the center's functioning, including a fundamental misalignment of mission and resources that the current director is seeking to rectify, the report concludes that the need for a DoD center focused on DMHA remains, but the center should focus, for now, on a subset of activities and missions. The report finds that while the Asia-Pacific represents a priority area for DMHA, because of the prevalence of disasters (about 45 percent of the global total) in that region, there is also a need for additional training, engagement, research, and information related to DMHA civil-military coordination in other regions, which a globally oriented center could provide and that the Office of the Secretary of Defense (OSD) should guide. Based on these conclusions, and after reviewing a number of courses of action, the report concludes that aligning CFE-DMHA with an existing globally oriented organization under OSD would best position the center to serve these purposes.

This research should be of interest to the many organizations, within and outside DoD, that are stakeholders of CFE-DMHA and are concerned with increasing its effectiveness in fulfilling its mandate of supporting and enhancing DoD's DMHA capacity.

Human subjects protection (HSP) protocols have been used in this report in compliance with U.S. Federal Policy for the Protection of Human Subjects and in accordance with the appropriate statutes and Department of Defense regulations governing HSP. The views of the anonymous sources cited in the report are solely their own and do not represent those of their organizations or the official policy or position of the Department of Defense, the United States Government, or any foreign government.

This research was sponsored by the Assistant Secretary of Defense for Special Operations/ Low-Intensity Conflict and conducted within the International Security and Defense Policy Center of the RAND National Defense Research Institute, a federally funded research and development center sponsored by the Office of the Secretary of Defense, the Joint Staff, the Unified Combatant Commands, the Navy, the Marine Corps, the defense agencies, and the defense Intelligence Community.

For more information on the International Security and Defense Policy Center, see www. rand.org/nsrd/ndri/centers/isdp or contact the director (contact information is provided on the web page).

Contents

Figures and Tables

Figures

Tables

Summary

In recognition of the important role that the U.S. military has to play in humanitarian assistance and disaster relief (HADR), congressional legislation established the Center for Excellence in Disaster Management and Humanitarian Assistance (CFE-DMHA) in Honolulu, Hawaii, in 1994. The center's initial missions were to provide and facilitate education, training, and research in civil-military operations in the international disaster management and humanitarian assistance (DMHA) arena; to make available high-quality disaster management and humanitarian assistance in response to disasters; to develop a repository of disaster-risk indicators for the Asia-Pacific region; and to perform other tasks as assigned by the Secretary of Defense.

The DMHA environment in which CFE-DMHA plans and conducts its activities has changed in a number of ways since its authorization. Foremost among these changes has been expansion in the number of U.S. and foreign agencies and organizations involved in disaster management, as well as improvements in their capabilities. In light of these changes, as well as the existence of some ambiguity in CFE-DMHA's institutional role in DMHA, the Assistant Secretary of Defense for Special Operations/Low-Intensity Conflict (ASD/SOLIC) asked RAND to review the roles and missions of CFE-DMHA.

When CFE-DMHA was established in 1994, its mission was assumed to be global. Since 2001, however, when CFE-DMHA was put under the administrative and operational control of the U.S. Pacific Command (PACOM), its focus has been primarily on the Asia-Pacific region, with a few short forays outside this region. While PACOM manages CFE-DMHA as a Direct Reporting Unit (DRU), the ASD/SOLIC exercises authority, direction, and control over CFE-DMHA through the CFE-DMHA director, the Joint Staff, and the commander of PACOM. The dual nature of authority over CFE-DMHA creates confusion, prevents the issuance of clear strategic guidance to CFE-DMHA, and suggests that command relationships should be clarified. Moreover, the questions remain of whether there are gaps in Department of Defense (DoD) capacity for DMHA in other regions and whether the changes in CFE-DMHA's landscape have increased requirements of the center.

This report examines CFE-DMHA's history and activities to help determine how the missions assigned by Congress can best be performed to meet the DMHA challenges facing DoD. This legislation is in large part ensconced in United States Code (U.S.C.), Title 10, Section 182, which authorizes CFE-DMHA to provide and facilitate education, training, and research in civil-military disaster-management operations (see Appendix A). For this study, RAND reviewed 400 documents and conducted 63 focused discussions, involving 66 individual subject-matter experts. (Some individuals participated in more than one discussion.) These experts represented organizations and experiences from across the U.S. and international DMHA spectrum, and included current and former staff of CFE-DMHA; relevant U.S.

government (USG) organizations, including the Office of the Secretary of Defense (OSD), PACOM, and other combatant commands; and other relevant foreign and international governmental or nongovernmental organizations (NGOs) working on DMHA or civil-military relations. The insights gained through these interviews and documents provided RAND with a wide range of important perspectives on CFE-DMHA's history, role, effectiveness, and potential future requirements.

The report examines the history of the center and reviews and assesses its performance. It reviews its various activities—including education and training, advise and assist efforts, engagements and exercises, and information sharing and research—and then the guidance, funding, manning, and other mission-support functions for these activities. The report examines three key questions facing CFE-DMHA: Which missions should it emphasize in the near term? Should CFE-DMHA focus on the Asia-Pacific, or should it be globally focused? And, based on the answers to these first two questions, what course of action makes the most sense for CFE-DMHA's missions and its geographic alignment?

A History Marked by Internal Challenges and Successive Reorientation

The history of CFE-DMHA is marked by major shifts in types of activities, scope of action, and mission focus. The center has changed from being heavily civilian oriented under its first two directors (1994–2008) to becoming a more military-oriented organization whose director is appointed by the PACOM commander and whose objectives many observers associate with those of the combatant command. These shifts were the result of the personal styles, backgrounds, and priorities of the center's successive directors; a lack of specific guidance to constrain these personal choices; and directors' efforts to pursue new areas of focus for additional funding in areas for which CFE-DMHA was not necessarily well suited. The shifts have resulted in difficulties for CFE-DMHA in establishing itself as a "brand" with a broadly recognizable set of missions and activities.

As CFE-DMHA has attempted to accommodate its expanding set of missions, PACOM and some CFE-DMHA directors have undertaken a number of attempts to improve CFE-DMHA's organizational structure and to provide the center with additional manpower. There have also been various proposals to combine the center with other organizations in Hawaii, such as the Asia-Pacific Center for Security Studies and the Pacific Disaster Center, or national military organizations, such as the National Defense University. Yet, throughout its 22-year history, the center has remained independent in attempting to navigate its broad mandate, with limited resources and oversight. But three key issues—internal administrative challenges, mandate not aligning with resources, and insufficient oversight and guidance—represent endemic problems for the center that should be addressed. With these problems in mind, the current director is proactively considering plans to mitigate these problems, but the resulting impact on the center's performance and stability remains to be seen.

An Assessment of the Center's Activities

CFE-DMHA needs a systematic process to assess its own performance and effectiveness. Performance assessment is a perennial challenge across DoD—and the United States government generally—and not specific to CFE-DMHA. Nevertheless, the center would greatly benefit from developing adequate metrics (including quantitative ones) to analyze and demonstrate to external audiences how it contributes to DoD and foreign-policy objectives, especially those for building foreign-partner capacity. Proper assessments would require dedicated staff and funds. In the absence of proper evaluation metrics specific to CFE-DMHA, this report relied heavily on documents and interviews to assess the center's activities.

Overall, CFE-DMHA's effectiveness as a DMHA organization is mixed. A number of its initiatives, particularly those designed to "follow the money" to determine CFE-DMHA programs or to attain a global posture, have not fared well and have negatively affected the center's reputation. Yet it does bring value in a number of important areas. One is training—of U.S. and foreign personnel and of civilians and military. CFE-DMHA's courses are well reviewed by participants, and the center has gained the trust of outside organizations to broaden its curriculum. CFE-DMHA also adds value to engagement efforts because of its ability to bridge the civil-military gap and to engage a variety of partners, including countries and organizations that are usually reluctant to associate with the U.S. military. CFE-DMHA's information sharing and research activities have garnered mixed reviews but seem to have improved in recent years and constitute the core of what is to be expected of a "center for excellence." To some extent, advising and assisting commanders during disaster response also falls into what a center for excellence should provide. CFE-DMHA staff participation in PACOM exercises, however, does not appear to be a unique contribution of CFE-DMHA; rather, much of its support seems to provide surge capacity to make up for manning shortages in PACOM, such as scenario development and role-playing. If exercise support continues, CFE-DMHA should approach exercises as an opportunity to evaluate partner-nation capacity (e.g., after-action teams) and strengthen regional engagement around shared DMHA interests (e.g., Association of Southeast Asian Nations Defence Ministers' Meeting Plus), as well as venues for education and training. In addition, CFE-DMHA should only focus on those activities where it brings the most value—for instance, limiting advise-and-assist activities to strategic decisionmakers rather than operational planners, or focusing its finite capacity for engagement only on those organizations and countries that have been defined as its highest strategic priorities.

We conclude that the center and the capabilities it brings to the DMHA environment should not be abolished. The need for such capabilities is likely only to increase with the number of disasters, both natural and man-made. CFE-DMHA has built some unique capabilities in its courses, research products, and relationships in the Asia-Pacific region that provide value to DoD and address important needs. CFE-DMHA is also particularly well positioned to engage both civilians and militaries, thanks to its special congressional authority, which would be lost if CFE-DMHA were to disappear. But CFE-DMHA's historical trajectory of dysfunction, lack of focus, and uneven effectiveness is likely to continue if the status quo is maintained. The current director has sought to make important progress in improving the operation and focus of CFE-DMHA, but our research suggests that the center's future success in meeting the needs of DoD and the humanitarian community depends on fundamental change in the center's form.

Is the Center Adequately Positioned to Execute Its Missions?

An examination of the center's guidance, funding, manning, and support functions shows that there is misalignment between the center's missions and its resources. This has been a perennial problem for CFE-DMHA and is a central element of the current director's plans to sharpen the center's focus. A review of its history and performance suggests a number of inadequacies that should be addressed regardless of the form the center takes in the future. CFE-DMHA's effectiveness would be greatly enhanced by the following six attributes:

- *Implementing guidance that defines roles and responsibilities.* Guidance to CFE-DMHA from OSD and, until recently, PACOM, has been infrequent and often vague. The offices overseeing the center should provide regular (at least annual) guidance that prioritizes the DMHA objectives that the center is to pursue over the following year but remains sufficiently flexible to allow response to emerging opportunities. The guidance must also define the roles and responsibilities of the director and his or her relationships with other stakeholders.

- *Consistent core funding over the long term.* Both core and supplemental funding for CFE-DMHA have been inconsistent, and together they have declined from about $10 million to $5.5 million since 2011. For CFE-DMHA, the ability to forge and maintain relationships between DoD and international organizations, NGOs, foreign-partner civilian agencies, and academic institutions requires consistent interaction, a solid foundation of planned activities and engagements, and flexibility. This requires consistent funding over the long term to ensure a continuing high level of activity with partners and to retain the expertise on staff to implement the activities.

- *Adequate mix of USG and contract employees.* The center retains a small cadre of USG employees and a four-to-one ratio of contractors to USG employees. A center seeking to appropriately represent official U.S. policy to foreign audiences and maintain efficient operations should have a more balanced workforce of contractors to USG employees. The center particularly needs more USG employees to engage in "inherently governmental" functions.

- *Widely recognized DMHA experts on staff with extensive and recent experience in civil-military coordination in disasters.* While it was beyond the scope of the present study to systematically evaluate the expertise of current CFE-DMHA staff, multiple discussants said that CFE-DMHA needs more staff with recent humanitarian and disaster experience and who are established experts in their fields. Only a very small number of CFE-DMHA staff members were recognized by name as interlocutors with other organizations.

- *A civilian "face" to the organization with staff who can maintain positive relationships with stakeholders, especially civilians and foreign partners.* A DoD disaster-management center that offers a civilian orientation builds trust more easily with foreign organizations and agencies, particularly international organizations and NGOs that are reluctant to work with the military. While CFE-DMHA continues to maintain a number of sensitive relationships, including with international organizations, its activities and command structure (including status as a PACOM DRU and directors who are active or retired military commanders) have been increasingly associated with military objectives that can complicate these relationships.

- *A director who, in order of priority, (1) is a proven, effective leader and manager; (2) has executive-level status; and (3) has experience in DMHA.* These qualities were mentioned consistently by discussants and are borne out by research in leadership. Hiring of the director should be open and competitive, with full coordination among the key stakeholders.

These are attributes that a functioning civil-military coordination entity such as CFE-DMHA requires to properly fulfill its mandate. If applied to CFE-DMHA, they would mitigate and, we hope, end the turbulence that has marked the center since its inception. The current CFE-DMHA acting director, a U.S. Air Force colonel, is already pursuing options to at least partially address many of these needs.

Conclusions and Recommendations: Missions, Geographic Focus, and Courses of Action

The form the center should take must be based on the missions it will emphasize (drawn from its congressional authority in Title 10) and its geographic focus.

CFE-DMHA should not equally emphasize all missions assigned to it in congressional legislation. At the same time, DoD should not seek to change CFE-DMHA–related statutes, because they allow for flexibility to address future missions that CFE-DMHA is not resourced or positioned to pursue now. The field of DMHA has benefited from the addition of a number of new players, including ones associated with DoD. As demand has grown, other organizations have stepped in to fill the capacity gap. The principal agencies (such as the U.S. Agency for International Development and the Defense Threat Reduction Agency) that perform these missions have greatly expanded their training and oversight of military activities in DMHA. Many missions assigned by Congress to CFE-DMHA are also performed at least in part by other organizations, at times with more resources. Moreover, CFE-DMHA has already reduced its activities in a number of these areas. Nevertheless, there are Title 10 missions assigned to CFE-DMHA whose associated demands have not been satisfied, where CFE-DMHA may have a competitive advantage, and where its role is unique, namely:

- *"Provide and facilitate education, training, and research in civil-military operations, particularly operations that require international disaster management and humanitarian assistance and operations that require coordination between the Department of Defense and other agencies"*—a broad mission that involves DMHA across multiple types of disasters.
- *"Provide and facilitate education, training, interagency coordination, and research on . . . [m]eeting requirements for information in connection with regional and global disasters, including the use of advanced communications technology as a virtual library"*—a mission that puts CFE-DMHA in the business of collecting, developing, disseminating, and archiving lessons learned and best practices.
- *"The Center shall perform such other missions as the Secretary of Defense may specify"*—a statement that allows CFE-DMHA to perform emerging missions as needed, such as researching the impact of climate change on military requirements.[1]

CFE-DMHA additionally should partially support the mission to "make available high-quality disaster management and humanitarian assistance in response to disasters" by providing advice and information to high-level commanders and foreign-partner organizations during contingencies.

---

[1] United States Code, Title 10, Sec. 182, Center for Excellence in Disaster Management and Humanitarian Assistance, January 3, 2012.

In Title 10, Section 182, Congress assigned missions to CFE-DMHA with the intention that most of them should be carried out globally. RAND's review of documents and discussions with multiple organizations and experts corroborate the need for an organization with a truly global outlook that advances civil-military coordination in DMHA to help meet requirements that are not being met at this time. While the Asia-Pacific should remain a primary focus because of its strategic importance for the Unites States, the prevalence of natural disasters, and the need to maintain important CFE-DMHA activities and relationships, there are broader needs that require CFE-DMHA's Title 10 authority to be executed globally. The common challenges that a globally oriented CFE-DMHA could address involve (1) a lack of coherent management of DMHA issues in some combatant commands; (2) inadequate education, training, and experience among DoD command staff and responding units; and (3) a lack of ready access to analytical products, including country baseline assessments or databases of lessons learned or best practices.

If CFE-DMHA is to fulfill these needs, OSD will need to reconfigure the center and provide it with the necessary guidance, resources, and organizational structure, according to the six attributes described above (in addition to an assessment process). A review of five courses of action for a future CFE-DMHA suggests that a merger with an existing, globally oriented DoD organization—such as the Naval Postgraduate School's Center for Civil Military Relations or the Pacific Disaster Center, though it was beyond our scope to analyze such organizations—would provide the course of action most likely to ensure CFE-DMHA's success in accomplishing its global missions. As important, such a merger could enhance CFE-DMHA's reputation for excellence and as a reliable partner in DMHA. Aligning CFE-DMHA with an existing, globally oriented DoD institution with overlapping activities would enable CFE-DMHA to adopt and share the host organization's culture and outlook, administrative functions, processes, and established networks and could leverage the host's reputation to enhance its own. CFE-DMHA would have a central core of DMHA staff (who may be physically located or virtually aligned with the host organization) and experts assigned to combatant commands as needed, with roles deconflicted from command staff functions, most of whom could reside in the PACOM area of responsibility in a "Pacific-first" approach, with reachback to the core.

CFE-DMHA is at a critical juncture in its 22-year history. It has been struggling for years to fulfill a mandate that one discussant described as "mile-wide" with limited resources. This makes it necessary for the center to focus on those areas that generate the greatest return on investment. Yet this is not likely to solve all of the issues that the center has been experiencing over the years. Despite some recent progress as a regionally focused center, CFE-DMHA should be reconfigured as a globally oriented center from which all of DoD can benefit in preparing for and responding to a wide range of disasters.

Acknowledgments

We are grateful for the support and help of many individuals. In particular, we would like to thank our principal sponsor and point of contact, Jennifer Smoak of the Office of Stability and Humanitarian Assistance, for her insight and guidance during many fruitful interactions, as well as her predecessor, Doug Stropes. We are thankful for the insights provided by Anne Witkowsky, Deputy Assistant Secretary of Defense for Stability and Humanitarian Assistance, and to Michael Lumpkin, Assistant Secretary of Defense for Special Operations/Low-Intensity Conflict. Colonel Joseph Martin, Acting Director of the Center for Excellence in Disaster Management and Humanitarian Assistance (CFE-DMHA), spent a great deal of time in very productive discussions with us throughout the course of the project and shared CFE-DMHA's archived documents with us. The current and former staff of CFE-DMHA also provided great insight and support, especially during our research trip to the organization. In addition, we would like to express appreciation to officials in U.S. Pacific Command for their support of our visit there and staff discussions, as well as the representatives of the many U.S., foreign, and international organizations who took the time to speak with us during this project and provided invaluable input into our research. Our thanks also go to David Hamon, who shared his expertise with us regarding disaster management and humanitarian responses.

We greatly appreciate the comments of Larry Hanauer and Bernd McConnell, who reviewed the initial draft of this report, significantly improving its quality and accuracy.

We are further indebted to our RAND colleagues who provided support and advice over the course of this project. Jennifer Moroney gave this study its initial impulse. Ryan Henry provided tremendously helpful insights along the way. Kyle Bertram, Erin Dick, Stacy Fitzsimmons, Whitney Heres, Lisa Turner, Francisco Walter, and Donna White helped with the research and editing of this report. A special thanks goes to our extraordinary communications analyst, Clifford Grammich, who was indispensable in the revision of the draft.

Of course, responsibility for the content of this report lies solely with the authors.

CHAPTER ONE

Introduction

The President's 2015 National Security Strategy calls for the U.S. military to be ready to mitigate the effects of natural disasters, both at home and abroad, and to be postured globally to "render humanitarian and disaster relief, and build the capacity of [U.S.] partners to join with [the United States] in meeting security challenges."[1] Disaster management and humanitarian assistance (DMHA), therefore, constitute an integral mission of the U.S. armed forces.

The understanding that the U.S. military has an important role to play in this field is not new. In recognition of the mission's importance, Congress established the Center for Excellence in Disaster Management and Humanitarian Assistance (CFE-DMHA) in Honolulu, Hawaii, in 1994, based on lessons learned in complex humanitarian emergencies that took place in the Balkans, the African Great Lakes region, Somalia, and the Middle East during the 1980s and early 1990s. CFE-DMHA was established to provide and facilitate education, training, and research in civil-military (civ-mil) operations, particularly operations that require international DMHA; to make available high-quality DMHA in response to disasters; develop a repository of disaster-risk indicators for the Asia-Pacific region; and other missions, as assigned by the Secretary of Defense. Congress assigned these missions to CFE-DMHA under Title 10 of the United States Code (U.S.C.), Section 182.[2] CFE-DMHA's chief benefactor, Senator Daniel Inouye of Hawaii, saw the development of a center of expertise in DMHA as highly beneficial not only to his state but also in the preparation for and mitigation of natural and man-made disasters worldwide. The congressional authority is relatively broad, and it allows CFE-DMHA, as a Department of Defense (DoD) entity to engage with foreign civilian organizations as a matter of course, something that is relatively unique in Title 10 security-cooperation authorities.

However, the environment in which CFE-DMHA plans and conducts its activities has changed in a number of ways in the past 22 years. At the time CFE-DMHA was conceived in the early 1990s, U.S. military response to disasters, interagency approaches, and coordination with international and nongovernmental organizations (NGOs) were generally ad hoc. Since the center's inception in 1994, the military's involvement in preparing for and responding to disasters and providing humanitarian assistance has become more systematic. In the past two decades, humanitarian assistance and disaster relief (HADR) has become a better-defined mission set within DoD, prompting the development of plans, leadership, organizations, exercises, and processes within the Office of the Secretary of Defense (OSD), the Joint

---

[1] Barack Obama, *National Security Strategy*, Washington, D.C.: White House, February 2015, p. 7.

[2] 10 U.S.C. 182, Center for Excellence in Disaster Management and Humanitarian Assistance, January 3, 2012. For the text of Title 10, Section 182, see Appendix A.

Staff, the defense agencies, and the combatant commands (CCMDs) dedicated to it. Moreover, Congress has provided tools, namely authorities and resources, to enable these more systematic efforts. While DoD views humanitarian assistance as an opportunity to contribute to U.S. government (USG) efforts to relieve the suffering of disaster victims, it also recognizes the benefits that may be gained, particularly via disaster preparedness and mitigation activities, through opportunities and relationships with countries and other partners that otherwise might be problematic to engage.

Coordination between DoD and other USG agencies, as well as between the USG and international organizations and NGOs, has also improved. For example, representatives from the Department of State's U.S. Agency for International Development (USAID) and its Office of Foreign Disaster Assistance (OFDA) are assigned to most geographic CCMDs to help ensure that the U.S. military's humanitarian-assistance efforts are well planned and synchronized during disaster-response operations. Interagency coordination has made a great deal of progress, as evidenced by the improved awareness and sophistication of combined U.S. efforts during the 2011 Tomodachi operation in the aftermath of the Japanese tsunami and nuclear disaster.[3] The military has also improved its efforts to engage with international organizations and with NGOs; while these organizations maintain some sensitivity to working with the U.S. military, DoD's understanding of this sensitivity has improved, in part because of CFE-DMHA's work.

At the same time, foreign governments, international organizations, and NGOs have dedicated efforts and resources to building capacity to prepare for, respond to, and manage disasters on their own. Nations in the Asia-Pacific, for example, are better prepared to respond to typhoons and other natural disasters and are less likely to call for help from the United States. A number of these governments have developed institutions similar to the U.S. domestic disaster agency, the Federal Emergency Management Agency (FEMA), and plan for and exercise their domestic and international disaster-response capabilities to capture lessons learned and best practices. At times, these activities are supported by the USG, including CFE-DMHA. In contrast with the situation two decades ago, many countries in the region are now able to handle all but the largest disasters without requesting outside help.[4]

Yet important needs remain, especially because there are signs that climate change is having a detrimental impact on the severity of natural disasters, and that man-made disasters are no less likely. According to the Centre for Research on the Epidemiology of Disasters, from 1990 to 2000, there were 5,917 reported natural and technological (i.e., large industrial and transport) disasters worldwide; from 2000 to 2010, this number increased 41 percent, to a reported 8,345 disasters.[5] According to NASA, climate change could increase the intensity of storms, including hurricanes and cyclones, and induce increased drought and flooding.[6] With projected increases in global population, urbanization, and economic growth, future

---

[3] Conversation with current or former HADR organization staff, 2015. See also Jennifer D. Moroney, Stephanie Pezard, Laurel E. Miller, Jeffrey Engstrom, and Abby Doll, *Lessons from Department of Defense Disaster Relief Efforts in the Asia-Pacific Region*, Santa Monica, Calif.: RAND Corporation, RR-146-OSD, 2013, pp. 85–107.

[4] Phone conversation with current or former CFE-DMHA staff, 2014. See also Alisa Tang, "After Decades of Disasters, U.N. Shifts Its Asia Operations," Reuters, June 29, 2015.

[5] The EM-DAT: The International Disaster Database (www.emdat.be) is available from the Centre for Research on the Epidemiology of Disasters, Université Catholique de Louvain, Brussels; these figures are from August 2015.

[6] Holli Riebeek, "The Rising Cost of Natural Hazards," NASA Earth Observatory, March 28, 2005.

disasters will affect more people and cause greater property damage, thereby potentially creating a higher level of instability throughout the world. Thus, the need for USG involvement in civ-mil coordination for disaster management and humanitarian assistance likely will remain despite the improvements over the past 20 years. In this changing landscape, however, it is important to ascertain whether the capabilities the United States can bring to bear—such as those ensconced in CFE-DMHA and the programs it offers to partners—are adequate to the task of preparing for future disasters and humanitarian crises.

Such a review is particularly important in the case of CFE-DMHA, because there has always been some ambiguity regarding its institutional role. The statute that established CFE-DMHA assumed that its mission would be global.[7] In 2001, however, CFE-DMHA was transferred to U.S. Pacific Command (PACOM) for administrative and operational control. Since that time, CFE-DMHA has focused primarily on the Asia-Pacific region, with only a few short forays into the broader global environment. While PACOM manages CFE-DMHA as a Direct Reporting Unit (DRU), the Assistant Secretary of Defense for Special Operations and Low-Intensity Conflict (ASD/SOLIC) exercises authority, direction, and control over CFE-DMHA through the CFE-DMHA director, the Joint Staff, and the commander of PACOM. However, according to DoD officials, without having financial or operational control, ASD/SOLIC lacks effective means to exercise authority and direction.[8] The dual nature of authority over CFE-DMHA suggests that command relationships should be further clarified. Moreover, the questions remain of whether there are gaps in DoD capacity for DMHA in other regions, and whether the changes in the landscape described above have changed the requirements levied on CFE-DMHA.

In light of presidential, DoD, and congressional guidance and the increasing instances of natural disasters that will require coordinated responses by the United States and its partners, it is therefore prudent to reexamine CFE-DMHA's role to determine whether it is postured appropriately to assist and enhance DoD's ability to meet the requirements of humanitarian crises in conjunction with partner nations.

This report explores CFE-DMHA's history and activities to help determine how the missions assigned to it in Title 10 can best be performed to meet the DMHA challenges facing DoD. The report concludes that a center focused on DMHA fulfills important needs that will only grow in the future and that CFE-DMHA should not be abolished. After coming to this conclusion, the report goes on to answer three key questions:

1. Which missions should CFE-DMHA emphasize in the near term?
2. Should CFE-DMHA be regionally focused on the Asia-Pacific, or should it be globally focused?
3. In light of the answers to the first two questions, which courses of action make the most sense for CFE-DMHA's mission and its geographic alignment?

The report recommends that the center focus, for now, on a subset of missions assigned to it in Title 10 and supporting activities. The report finds that while the Asia-Pacific presents a large proportion of the global challenge in preparing for and managing natural disasters, because of their prevalence in the region, there is a need for additional training, engagement, research,

---

[7] Phone conversation with current or former CFE-DMHA staff, 2014.

[8] Comments from DoD officials, March 16, 2016.

and information related to DMHA civ-mil coordination in other regions, which a globally oriented center could provide and that OSD should guide. Based on these conclusions, and after reviewing a number of courses of action, the report concludes that OSD should seek to align CFE-DMHA with an existing globally oriented organization to best position the center to serve these purposes.

Methodology and Organization of the Report

To conduct the research for this study, RAND reviewed 400 documents and conducted 63 focused discussions involving 66 individual subject-matter experts (SMEs); some individuals participated in more than one discussion; some discussions involved more than one individual. These experts represented organizations and experiences from across the U.S. and international DMHA spectrum and included current and former staff of

- CFE-DMHA
- DoD and other USG organizations working on DMHA or civ-mil relations, including the CCMDs and especially PACOM
- international organizations, NGOs, and a foreign civ-mil coordination agency.[9]

The insights gained through these interviews and document review provided RAND with a wide range of important perspectives on CFE-DMHA's history, role, effectiveness, and potential future requirements. Throughout this document, interlocutors are cited in very general terms to secure their identities.

Chapter Two provides a concise history of CFE-DMHA and describes both the accomplishments and challenges that have surrounded the center during its 22-year existence. Chapter Three then assesses CFE-DMHA performance on major activities using qualitative insights from the discussions and, in a small number of cases, quantitative measures from documentation RAND reviewed. Building on the review of CFE-DMHA history and activities, Chapter Four addresses the three questions above and provides recommendations for a way ahead for the center. Chapter Five summarizes the report's findings and recommendations. Appendix A provides the language of Title 10, Section 182, as well as its amendments, while Appendix B presents a concept by which a future center might assess its activities and track progress in delivering DMHA effects to support DoD objectives.

---

[9]   The breakdown of discussants is as follows: 20 current or former CFE-DMHA staff, ten current or former PACOM officials, eight other CCMDs officials, 13 current or former other USG staff, and 15 current or former staff of other HADR organizations.

CHAPTER TWO

The History of CFE-DMHA

Since its establishment in 1994, CFE-DMHA has struggled, as a small organization with limited resources, to undertake the broad set of missions under its mandate. Changes in the international environment, shifts in the direction taken by CFE-DMHA leadership, and a lack of oversight have further complicated the center's ability to develop a consistent set of actions or activities.

Throughout this report, we refer to *missions* assigned to CFE-DMHA by Congress under Title 10 legislation and the *activities* that CFE-DMHA conducts in support of those missions. The activities we address are based on a categorization that CFE-DMHA has used in analysis of its areas of focus.[1] Table 2.1 provides a "crosswalk" between the activity categories and CFE-DMHA's Title 10 missions (which are paraphrased from the original congressional language provided in Appendix A).

Education and training, engagements and exercises, advise and assist activities, and information sharing are activities relevant to almost all missions. Two missions, disaster response (mission 2) and risk indicators for the Asia-Pacific (mission 4), focus on more-narrow activities (advise and assist for mission 2 and information sharing—which includes research—for missions 2 and 4). Conversely, the advise-and-assist activity category does not appear to be relevant to Mission 1. In Chapters Two, Three, and Four, we refer to these activities and supported missions to describe and assess CFE-DMHA's past and present efforts and to frame recommended courses of action for the future. We begin by reviewing the history of CFE-DMHA and the evolution of its missions.

1994–2000: The Genesis of the Center for Excellence—An Academic-Based Organization with a Broad Mission

CFE-DMHA was established in 1994 with a broad mission to improve civ-mil coordination to respond to the growing number of humanitarian disasters requiring U.S. military assistance. Recognizing the challenges the military faced providing aid to disaster victims in Iraq, Somalia, Bangladesh, and Hawaii,[2] U.S. Senator Daniel Inouye proposed the creation of the Disaster Management Training program to serve as a "center of excellence in training educa-

---

[1] CFE-DMHA, *Strategy to Task Analysis*, briefing, August 22, 2014b.

[2] These included Hurricane Iniki in September 1992, the deadliest and costliest hurricane to ever strike Hawaii. Cyclone Marian in Bangladesh in 1991 (which led to the U.S. Operation Sea Angel) and humanitarian crises in northern Iraq in 1992 (which led to Operation Provide Comfort) and in Somalia in 1992–1993 (which led to Operation Restore Hope).

Table 2.1
Crosswalk Between CFE-DMHA Activity Categories and Its Title 10 Missions

Title 10 CFE-DMHA Mission	Activity Category			
	Education and Training	Engagements and Exercises	Advise and Assist	Information Sharing
(1) Provide/facilitate education, training, and research on international civ-mil DMHA operations	√	√		√
(2) Make available high-quality DMHA in response to disasters			√	√
(3) Provide/facilitate education, training, interagency coordination, and research on: (3)(A) CBRN consequence management	√	√	√	√
(3)(B) Terrorism consequence management	√	√	√	√
(3)(C) Appropriate DMHA roles for reserve components	√	√	√	√
(3)(D) Information requests, including advanced communications technology for virtual library	√	√	√	√
(3)(E) Tropical medicine, particularly DoD medical readiness	√	√	√	√
(4) Develop repository of disaster risk indicators for the Asia-Pacific				√
(5) Other missions as the Secretary of Defense may specify	√	√	√	√

NOTE: CBRN = chemical, biological, radiological, and nuclear.

tion and research."[3] Inouye's legislation provided $1 million for the development of the program to be based at the Pacific Regional Medical Command's Tripler Army Medical Center, in partnership with the University of Hawaii and PACOM. The program, initially referred to as a "center of excellence," was proposed as a joint effort, which would use "the partnership's pooled resources and expertise [to] prepare DoD personnel to meet the requirements of operations other than war, including disaster relief and humanitarian assistance."[4] Based on this original legislative language, CFE-DMHA was formed as a research-based center of excellence for the purpose of collaborating with academia on evolving DMHA challenges.

While Congress did not initially stipulate the types of missions or activities that CFE-DMHA was intended to pursue, the center's first director, Dr. Frederick "Skip" Burkle, played a major role in determining the early focus of the organization. Burkle, who was appointed director in 1994, was a professor of emergency medicine at the University of Hawaii and had previously served as a civ-mil liaison during humanitarian operations Iraq and Somalia. He had a major role in founding the center and determining its initial focus. He envisioned an aca-

---

[3]   National Defense Authorization Act Fiscal Year 1994, Senate Conference Report for House Resolution 2401, January 1993, p. 356.

[4]   The first official reference to CFE-DMHA was in National Defense Authorization Act Fiscal Year 1994, 1993, p. 356. (While the three partner organizations were clearly focused on the PACOM area of responsibility, the legislative language did not indicate that the program would be as well.)

demically oriented center focused on education and training and information-sharing activities aimed at improving civ-mil coordination. Burkle emphasized the center's role as a collaborative entity, intent on building partnerships among the military, civilian, and nongovernmental agencies and facilitating integrated research on complex humanitarian emergencies, particularly in the area of public health.

Public health became a primary mission area during Burkle's tenure. Under his leadership, CFE-DMHA partnered with the Centers for Disease Control and Prevention (CDC) and became a World Health Organization Collaborating Centre, through which it conducted a number of health-related engagements.[5] CFE-DMHA also provided tailored health and disaster-response training programs for U.S. military personnel, such as Combined Humanitarian Assistance Response Training (CHART) and Health Emergencies in Large Populations (H.E.L.P.) courses, and published research papers on public-health issues. In addition to these health efforts, CFE-DMHA initiated a number of information-sharing activities, including the Virtual Information Center, the Pacific Disaster Management Information Network (PDMIN), and the Combined Event Notification Technology and Unified Reporting (CENTAUR) program, which focused more broadly on disaster-management coordination.[6] In 1999, the center introduced *Liaison*, a quarterly publication for sharing lessons learned on humanitarian assistance and disaster-relief efforts.[7]

As Burkle was expanding CFE-DMHA's involvement in health, education, research, and information-sharing activities, Inouye initiated an effort to obtain wider authority for it by shepherding legislation through Congress that placed the center in U.S.C. in 1997, under Title 10, Section 182. This new legislation codified CFE-DMHA's mission "to provide and facilitate education, training, and research in international DMHA and operations that require coordination between DoD and other agencies" and expanded its mandate to engage in a wide range of mission areas, including tropical medicine; nuclear, biological, and chemical events; consequences of terrorism; and the development of a repository of disaster-risk indicators for the Asia-Pacific region (see Table 2.1 and Appendix A).[8] The legislation also appeared to give the center a global mandate to engage in most DMHA activities; indeed, the Asia-Pacific region was mentioned only once, in reference to providing a repository of disaster-risk indicators. In 1998, Congress provided CFE-DMHA with an additional and unique authority to accept donations from any USG agency, foreign government, foundation, charitable organization, or private source (an authority that was rarely pursued).[9] In 1999, Congress allowed the

---

[5] The CDC became the fourth collaborating partner of CFE-DMHA, in addition to the Pacific Regional Medical Command at Tripler, PACOM, and the University of Hawaii. The CDC provided a full-time program manager and research physician and a half-time disaster specialist as "seconded staff" and led CFE-DMHA's dedicated public-health effort until September 2001, when CDC staff members were reassigned. Center of Excellence for Disaster Management and Humanitarian Assistance (COE-DMHA), *1998 Annual Report*, Honolulu, undated-a; COE-DMHA, *1999 Annual Report*, Honolulu, undated-b; and COE-DMHA, *2001 Mid-Year Activity Report*, Honolulu, 2002. Note that the center was previously named Center *of* Excellence for Disaster Management and Humanitarian Assistance.

[6] The Virtual Information Center was developed with PACOM. PDMIN was used to share information across government agencies and NGOs. CENTAUR includes foreign partners. COE-DMHA, undated-a.

[7] COE-DMHA, undated-b.

[8] Title 10, Section 182, was introduced into U.S.C. by Public Law 105–85, Title III, Sec. 382, Center for Excellence in Disaster Management and Humanitarian Assistance, November 18, 1997.

[9] Some efforts to secure donations were attempted under the directorships of Peter Bradford and LtGen. John Goodman between 2005 and 2012 but were ultimately unsuccessful. Phone conversation with current or former CFE-DMHA staff,

center to pay the expenses of foreign personnel engaged in disaster management, education, and training.

While Congress expanded CFE-DMHA's mission set, it did not designate a guaranteed source of funding. The center continued to operate as a partnership among PACOM, the University of Hawaii, the Tripler Medical Center, and the CDC. An advisory committee, consisting of the leaders of these four agencies and Inouye, provided only limited oversight and did not meet regularly after 1995.[10] Core funding was provided through annual congressional earmarks, funneled through the Pacific Regional Medical Command. Additional financial support was provided by the geographic CCMDs or other agencies, such as USAID or the Asia Pacific Regional Initiative (APRI), for programs or engagements conducted on their behalf. Yet CFE-DMHA had little control or accountability over its budget, because all its funding went through Tripler, and the distribution of its resources was controlled by the leadership of the Pacific Medical Command. Problems arising from control and accountability challenges have led to internal administrative problems throughout CFE-DMHA's history.[11]

It is important to note that CFE-DMHA did not launch into any new mission areas in 1997 in response to the codification of Section 182. Under Burkle's leadership, the center did not become engaged in terrorism-consequence management, for example, but only became more active in the areas in which it was already engaged (primarily education, training, and information-sharing activities for civ-mil operations and public health research). The center's level of activities still increased, yet its administrative staff remained limited. In 1995, it had only five personnel, consisting of one government employee, one military employee, and three contractors. Over the next four years, it hired additional contractors, but its core staff never exceeded three civilian or military employees. This limited level of staffing and small ratio of government to contractor employees limited the center's ability to address inherently governmental functions, which can only be fulfilled by USG employees.[12]

The combination of limited staffing, reliance on various outside funding sources, and lack of administrative control over its finances made program accounting difficult.[13] While the center was able to expand the number and reach of its education, training, and research programs (although not nearly as far as Title 10 allowed), its administrative capacity did not increase in proportion to its growth.[14] A lack of oversight and direction from CFE-DMHA's advisory committee also caused friction between the components of the center over the allo-

---

2015.

[10] The committee met actively from October 1994 to September 1995 but did not meet regularly thereafter. COE-DMHA, undated-a.

[11] It was beyond the scope of this study to explore the legal ramifications of these challenges.

[12] Title 31, Section 501, defines as "inherently governmental" "a function that is so intimately related to the public interest as to require performance by Federal Government employees. . . . The term includes activities that require either the exercise of discretion in applying Federal Government authority or the making of value judgments in making decisions for the Federal Government, including judgments relating to monetary transactions and entitlements" (U.S.C., Title 31, Sec. 501, Office of Management and Budget, 2011).

[13] Phone conversation with current or former CFE-DMHA staff, 2015.

[14] The CFE-DMHA staff did not initially include a comptroller. The Pacific Medical Command, while given responsibility for funding, had little financial oversight.

cation of resources. A DoD audit in February 2000 found the center to have poor financial management.[15]

2000–2008: Developing a More Operational Focus

Following Burkle's departure, the structure and focus of CFE-DMHA changed, yet many of the internal challenges the organization faced in meeting its broad mandate with limited resources and manpower remained. The Under Secretary of Defense for Policy (USD/P) assumed program and policy oversight authority in April 2000 and called on PACOM to assume operational control.[16] USD/P gave ASD/SOLIC responsibility for overseeing CFE-DMHA policy, guidance, and resources, while the PACOM commander was authorized to appoint the center's director. A year later, the PACOM's administrative role was strengthened as CFE-DMHA became a DRU under PACOM and began to receive funding through PACOM from the Navy's operations and maintenance (O&M) account.

These structural changes had little impact on the level of funding that CFE-DMHA received, however. Core funding continued to be determined by annual congressional earmarks, which were not guaranteed and never exceeded $5 million, while supplemental financial support remained dependent on the varying availability of external sources and grants. Staffing levels varied as a result. The number of government and military staff remained minimal, ranging from three to six in total, making the organization highly dependent on contractor support. Such small numbers of permanent staff made it difficult to perform the administrative functions required of a federally funded organization and were inadequate for an agency with such a wide range of activities and broad mandate. (See Chapter Three.)

The appointment of a new director of CFE-DMHA by PACOM in 2000, and the changing focus of U.S. national security interests, however, did have a decisive impact on types of missions that CFE-DMHA pursued. The center's second director, Gerard "Pete" Bradford III, assumed his position after serving as the director for operations of USAID/OFDA. Like Burkle, Bradford had a strong interest in promoting civ-mil collaboration for disaster response but favored operational engagement activities with NGOs over information sharing. He sought to increase the center's involvement in advise-and-assist activities that were directly involved in aiding disaster victims. Working more closely with PACOM, he enabled the center to become involved in providing support for exercises on pandemic response, for example, but no longer pursued public-health research. Under Bradford's leadership, CFE-DMHA continued to provide CHART and H.E.L.P. humanitarian response and health courses, but education did not receive as much emphasis.[17]

Following the September 11, 2001, terrorist attacks against the United States, CFE-DMHA expanded into new mission areas. The center became engaged in the consequences of terrorism with the development of terrorism-response training programs and adopted a

---

[15] Phone conversation with current or former CFE-DMHA staff, 2015; conversation with current or former CFE-DMHA staff, 2015.

[16] U.S. Secretary of Defense, memorandum establishing authority over CFE-DMHA under both PACOM and ASD/SOLIC, April 24, 2000.

[17] COE-DMHA, *Fiscal Year 2001 Annual Report*, Honolulu, undated-d; conversation with current or former HADR organization staff, 2015; and conversation with current or former CFE-DMHA staff, 2015.

new mission of peacekeeping operation training.[18] These efforts conformed to increasing national-security interests in capacity-building efforts with nontraditional foreign partners. In 2002, "CFE's mission offer[ed] a low profile tool to engage civilian and military communities throughout the theater that might otherwise be hesitant to work with us . . . by promoting broader collaboration among non-traditional partners; CFE contribute[d] to the creation of an environment less hospitable to terrorism."[19] To enable the center to support the training of nontraditional partners, Congress in October 2002 allowed the center to pay for the training of military and civilian personnel of foreign countries in disaster management, peace operations, and humanitarian assistance.[20] This ability to use Title 10 funds to support the training of civilians provided CFE-DMHA with a new and unique capability in DoD.

Most CFE-DMHA programs during Bradford's tenure focused on the Pacific region, although center staff continued to participate in international workshops and programs and to engage in humanitarian-assistance operations globally, particularly in Iraq and Pakistan. The center was closely tied to PACOM as a DRU, yet it still operated independently in its programming, often pursuing outside funding sources, such as the Enhanced International Peacekeeping Capabilities (EIPC) program, to support its activities. Bradford sought to maintain CFE-DMHA autonomy from PACOM to maintain a perception of neutrality and to enable the center to be a bridge between civilian and military organizations.[21] CFE-DMHA leadership resisted a 2006 OSD proposal, known as the "Hawaii model," to merge with the Asia-Pacific Center for Security Studies (APCSS) and the Pacific Disaster Center (PDC) and place all three organizations under the operational control of the Defense Security Cooperation Agency (DSCA), because of the belief that such a merger would compromise CFE-DMHA's ability to work with NGOs and restrict its access in countries where the U.S. military was not welcome.[22] Center leaders were also hesitant about being absorbed by a new DoD bureaucracy.[23]

The center's independence became somewhat more constrained in 2008, when CFE-DMHA became a Program of Record in the PACOM budget and no longer received separate funding through congressional earmarks.[24] This provided PACOM with greater influence over CFE-DMHA's core funding and resulted in more competition for resources. It also led to renewed internal dysfunction over the distribution of program funds.[25] Although CFE-DMHA remained a separate entity, its ability to set its own course and function administratively was limited by the end of Bradford's term in 2008.

---

[18] New peacekeeping programs included the Asia-Pacific Peace Operations Capacity Building Program and the EIPC program, which was developed with the Center for Civil Military Relations. COE-DMHA, 2002.

[19] Dennis C. Blair, "Statement of Admiral Dennis C. Blair, U.S. Navy Commander in Chief, U.S. Pacific Command, before a Subcommittee of the Committee on Appropriations," U.S. Senate, 107th Congress, Special Hearing, April 3, 2002.

[20] Public Law 107-248, Appropriations for the Department of Defense for Fiscal Year 2003, Sec. 8093, October 23, 2002.

[21] Conversation with current or former CFE-DMHA staff, 2015; conversation with current or former HADR organization staff, 2015; and conversation with current or former CFE-DMHA staff, 2015.

[22] Phone conversation with current or former CFE-DMHA staff, 2015.

[23] Phone conversation with current or former CFE-DMHA staff, 2015.

[24] In fiscal year (FY) 2008, CFE-DMHA became a Program of Record in the PACOM budget under Operation and Maintenance of the Navy, 1C6C Combat Support Forces Department of the Navy, Operation and Maintenance, Navy 1C6C Combat Support Forces FY 2008 President's Budget Submission Exhibit OP-5; and phone conversation with current or former CFE-DMHA staff, 2015; and others.

[25] Phone conversation with current or former CFE-DMHA staff, 2015.

2008–2012: Shifting to the Military and a More Global Posture

CFE-DMHA became more closely aligned with PACOM and the wider defense community during the tenure of its third director, LtGen. (Ret.) John Goodman. Goodman had previously served as the commander of the Pacific Marine Forces and commanded Joint Task Force Caring Response following Cyclone Nargis in Burma in May 2008. Under his leadership, the center engaged less with international organizations and NGOs, and shifted its efforts toward building the capacity of the U.S. military and partner nations to respond to humanitarian disasters and develop greater resiliency.[26] At the same time, he also attempted to give the center a more global posture.

While CFE-DMHA remained involved in education and training, engagements and exercises, advise-and-assist, and information-sharing activities, as it had under Bradford, the focus of these types of activities changed. Humanitarian Assistance Response Training (HART) and H.E.L.P. courses continued but were adapted for different countries.[27] The center also engaged in more programs to train partner-nation militaries.[28] This effort to provide disaster-management training to foreign militaries corresponded with the key components of the 2010 Quadrennial Defense Review, which established the building of security capacity of partner nations as a key mission and placed particular emphasis on building the capacity to respond to humanitarian crises and natural disasters among U.S. partners in the Asia-Pacific region.[29]

CFE-DMHA provided SMEs to help with humanitarian-assistance operations in PACOM, such as Operation Tomodachi in Japan, but also made an effort to engage more globally, such as Operation Unified Response in Haiti. Additionally, the center launched a new effort to send liaisons to the U.S. Northern Command (NORTHCOM), U.S. European Command (EUCOM), and Washington, D.C., to engage more consistently outside the PACOM area of responsibility (AOR). Moreover, CFE-DMHA, under Goodman's leadership, promoted a global effort to pursue the Title 10 authorized mission to develop a repository of disaster-risk indicators by developing a computer-based disaster-risk indicator model, known as The Resiliency Analysis and Coordination System (TRACS). This model was intended to enable geographic combatant commanders to determine a partner nation's risk vulnerability and to guide its disaster-response and security-cooperation plans. The adoption of a more global focus by CFE-DMHA received formal support from USD/P in a policy memo to the geographic CCMDs in 2010, which stipulated that CFE-DMHA supported all CCMDs as a DoD source for HADR concepts, education, and training.[30]

---

[26] Phone conversation with current or former CFE-DMHA staff, 2015; and COE-DMHA, *2010 Command History, Annex J to U.S. Pacific Command History, 1 January–31 December 2010*, Honolulu, 2010.

[27] Phone conversation with former CFE-DMHA staff, 2015.

[28] The focus on pandemic-response programs was attributed to Goodman's past experience leading PACOM's Consequence Support Force 503 in its response to the avian influenza pandemic.

[29] In referring to U.S. military objectives in the Pacific, the Quadrennial Defense Review stated: "We will augment regional deterrence and rapid response capabilities and seek opportunities to build the capacity of our Asian partners to respond more effectively to contingencies, including humanitarian crises and natural disasters." U.S. Department of Defense, *Quadrennial Defense Review Report*, Washington, D.C., February 2010.

[30] In a 2010 policy memo from the Under Secretary of Defense for Policy to CCMDs, CFE-DMHA was requested to provide expertise to all of the geographic CCMDs and specified areas in which CFE-DMHA could assist in theater security cooperation efforts. The memo also encouraged the CCMDs to utilize CFE-DMHA as a resource. COE-DMHA, *Business Case Analysis*, manpower review briefing, Ford Island, Hawaii, November 2012c.

CFE-DMHA did not receive significantly more resources to support its global mission. From 2008 to 2010, its budget actually decreased by more than 15 percent, while staffing, which a PACOM analysis had determined to be insufficient for the center's mission, increased only slightly, from 34 to 38 personnel.[31] A subsequent 2011 report by the PACOM inspector general concluded that the center needed additional manpower to ensure compliance with DoD program directives, yet, while increasing to 43 in 2011, staffing fell again to 31 in 2012 and continued to consist primarily of more costly contracted employees—limiting CFE-DMHA's ability to address inherently governmental functions among its expanded responsibilities.[32] While the PACOM commander signed a September 2011 memorandum of understanding (MOU) with the CFE-DMHA director stating that PACOM was the center's "primary customer" and the command would provide the center with guidance on how to balance its support requests with those from other CCMDs, this balance was difficult to maintain with limited resources and staffing, and especially with CFE-DMHA's funding coming through PACOM.

Interestingly, Goodman's efforts to establish a presence beyond PACOM met with resistance from the staff at the other geographic commands, raising questions about the value of CFE-DMHA's global initiatives. Problems arose over the roles and cost-sharing arrangements of CFE-DMHA liaisons in EUCOM and of their roles in NORTHCOM; both liaisons were gone by 2011. A parallel attempt to engage a liaison in the U.S. Africa Command (AFRICOM) was rebuffed by the AFRICOM staff.[33] Support for TRACS among the geographic commands declined because questions were raised about the utility of the program and the manpower and resources required for its development.[34]

To obtain greater support for CFE-DMHA's global mission, Goodman engaged in preliminary discussions with ASD/SOLIC regarding the possibility of incorporating the center under the auspices of the National Defense University and the DSCA. While the proposal reportedly received initial support from the National Defense University, bureaucratic hurdles among PACOM, CFE-DMHA, and a new university leadership prevented the option from being pursued.[35] By early 2012, uncertainty over the scope of CFE-DMHA's mission, disagreements among its staff over the types of activities to pursue, and accusations of mismanagement were impeding the good functioning of the organization.

---

[31] CFE-DMHA, "CFE Manpower-Task Comparison," briefing slides, internal document, Ford Island, Hawaii, undated-c, slide 1.

[32] COE-DMHA, "COE-DMHA: Manpower Review Briefing," briefing slides, internal document, Honolulu, November 21, 2012b, referencing a study carried out by PACOM's Inspector General (IG).

[33] The CFE-DMHA liaison in NORTHCOM reportedly resigned after one year. In EUCOM, there were problems concerning the role and shared cost of liaison personnel between the two organizations, as well as allegations of failure to fulfill contract terms. U.S. Europe Command and the CFE-DMHA, memorandum of agreement, Revision 1, October 6, 2011; interview with current or former HADR staff, 2014; phone conversation with current or former CFE-DMHA staff, 2015; phone conversation with current or former CFE-DMHA staff, 2015; and conversation with current or former HADR organization staff, 2014.

[34] Questions arose over the utility of TRACS and its value relative to the significant funding invested in its development. Conversation with current or former HADR organization staff, 2015; conversation with current or former DoD official, 2014; and phone conversation with current or former AFRICOM official, 2015.

[35] In 2011, National Defense University President Nancy McEldowney supported the idea of moving CFE-DMHA within the university, but this option was not pursued. A similar proposal by DSCA was also dismissed (phone conversation with current or former CFE-DMHA staff, 2015).

2012–2014: Three Directors in Three Years

From 2012 to 2014, CFE-DMHA struggled to redefine its focus and organizational structure under the leadership of three consecutive directors with different visions of the center's direction. In February 2012, COL Philip Mead began a ten-month tenure as interim director as PACOM conducted a business case analysis (BCA) of CFE-DMHA's missions, roles, and responsibilities. The analysis concluded that the center's strength was in its ability to prepare U.S. forces for conducting HADR operations. It further suggested that the center should focus its efforts on meeting PACOM requirements, rather than expending its limited resources to support other CCMDs or to pursue a global mandate.[36] The BCA proposed a change in the center's personnel structure to reduce its reliance on contractors, recommending that the center be allowed to increase its number of government employee positions (or billets) and be granted excepted service hiring authority to recruit employees with particular subject-matter expertise.[37] Finally, the BCA provided three potential courses of action for the future structure of the center: (1) folding CFE-DMHA into PACOM (specifically PACOM's J7 Exercise Directorate), (2) folding CFE-DMHA into the APCSS, or (3) maintaining CFE-DMHA as an independent center.[38]

The PACOM commander endorsed most of the BCA's recommendations, noting that they corresponded with a strategic U.S. "rebalance" to Asia and the command's decision to make HADR a cornerstone of engagement with its allies and partners in the region.[39] In late 2012, in a decision memo, PACOM approved the organizational changes, authorized an additional 15 government positions, and supported the decision to keep the center as an independent DRU.[40] A few months later, however, the imposition of sequestration prevented an increase in CFE-DMHA manpower.[41]

Still, by the end of 2012, there was a noted change in CFE-DMHA, away from its global focus under Goodman and toward concentrating on activities that supported PACOM's theater-campaign plan. The center continued to engage in education and training activities through its HART courses (successor to the CHART program) but began tailoring the courses

---

[36] The BCA also recommended that the CFE-DMHA mission statement note that CFE-DMHA serves as DoD's and PACOM's "premier international humanitarian assistance and disaster management organization, (that) enhances civil-military preparedness and response through collaborative partnerships, applied research, best practices, and education and training." This mission statement was approved by PACOM in May 2012. COE-DMHA, *Business Case Analysis*, briefing, internal document, Ford Island, Hawaii, May 2012a.

[37] Federal government civilian positions are generally hired through a competitive process; however, the Office of Personnel Management provides excepted service hiring authorities to enable agencies to fill special jobs (often those requiring specialized expertise) when it is not feasible to use traditional competitive hiring procedures. The BCA also recommended that the center be granted excepted service hiring authority for recruiting SMEs to support its programs, but this proposal was not endorsed by PACOM. U.S. Office of Personnel Management, *Delegated Examining Operations Handbook: A Guide for Federal Agency Examining Offices*, Washington, D.C., May 2007; Phil Mead, *COE-DMHA Strategy and Organization Decision Brief*, Ford Island, Hawaii: Center for Excellence in Disaster Management and Humanitarian Assistance, September 18, 2011.

[38] COE-DMHA, 2012a.

[39] The CFE-DMHA's BCA also dovetailed with a PACOM J00 analysis that called for significant increases in staffing.

[40] Although the CFE-DMHA director recommended folding CFE-DMHA into APCSS, the PACOM commander, ADM Samuel Locklear, reportedly preferred to maintain the center as an independent entity. Phone conversation with current or former CFE-DMHA staff, 2015.

[41] Phone conversation with current or former CFE-DMHA staff, 2014.

to meet the specific needs of PACOM personnel. It sent SMEs to assist in PACOM exercises and engaged in security-cooperation engagement activities with regional organizations in the PACOM AOR.[42] CFE-DMHA also engaged in advise-and-assist and information-sharing activities, which were more focused on the Pacific region but conducted less frequently. New engagements depended on the level of funding available from outside sources, such as the USAID fund for influenza pandemic or the President's Emergency Plan for AIDS Relief, which provided short-term support for specific health-related missions.[43] As a result, the focus of CFE-DMHA's activities was increasingly determined by the availability of funding, rather than its core missions. During Mead's short tenure, CFE-DMHA's budget decreased nearly 20 percent, from $10.11 million in 2011 to $8.3 million in 2012, and the number of staff decreased to 31, of whom 19 were contractors.[44]

Pam Milligan, who became the center's fifth director, in January 2013, faced ongoing resource and personnel challenges.[45] Milligan, who had previously served as the chief of staff for PACOM's Operations Directorate as a brigadier general in the U.S. Air Force Reserves, conducted her own strategic reassessment of CFE-DMHA, in 2013, concluding that the center should attempt to address the broad range of activities called for in its Title 10, Section 182, missions.[46] Under Milligan's leadership, the center expanded its education programs to include training for CBRN disasters, a mission area that had not previously received much emphasis at CFE-DMHA. It engaged in more information-sharing activities through the launch of a new initiative to collect lessons learned about disasters. Moreover, it pursued the development of a new disaster-management preparedness collaboration tool that could provide a common operating picture of disaster-preparedness training activities to civilian and military organizations (along the lines of the mission to develop a repository of disaster-risk indicators). Nevertheless, progress on these initiatives was constrained by a continuing decrease of core funding, from $8.3 million in 2012 to $6.3 million in 2013.

CFE-DMHA struggled in its effort to assume a global mission during Milligan's tenure. In October 2013, the ASD/SOLIC reiterated guidance requiring the center to provide education and training, disaster-management assistance, and research to the global community, as well as to prepare to manage DoD's Civil-Military Emergency Preparedness Program (CMEP).[47] Assuming responsibility for CMEP, a Warsaw Initiative Fund (WIF) program that focused on

---

[42] Center for Excellence in Disaster and Humanitarian Assistance, *Organizational History, 1 January–31 December 2012,* Ford Island, Hawaii, 2013.

[43] Phone conversation with current or former CFE-DMHA staff, 2015; phone conversation with current or former CFE-DMHA staff, 2015.

[44] In November 2012, CFE-DMHA's staff temporarily fell to as low as 12, after the departure of CACI contractors. While the contractors were replaced, this turnover disrupted CFE-DMHA activities.

[45] Milligan served as an interim director of CFE-DMHA from January to May 2013 and as director from May 2013 to May 2014.

[46] Center for Excellence for Disaster Management and Humanitarian Assistance Strategy, *Strategy FY2014–2018,* Ford Island, Hawaii, January 2014a.

[47] OSD guidance required CFE-DMHA to prepare to manage the CMEP in FY 2014. U.S. Assistant Secretary of Defense, Office of Special Operations/Low-Intensity Conflict, "Memorandum for Commander, U.S. Pacific Command; Subject: Policy Guidance for Center for Excellence in Disaster Management and Humanitarian Assistance (CFE)," October 18, 2013.

former Soviet bloc countries[48] required further expansion of the center's operations beyond the PACOM AOR and presented CFE-DMHA with significant legal and financial challenges.[49]

OSD's decision to move CMEP to CFE-DMHA was based on its desire to leverage the center's special authority to conduct engagements with both military and civilian agencies. Most DoD agencies, including the U.S. Army Corps of Engineers, which had previously managed CMEP, are prohibited from engaging nonmilitary entities without special authority.[50] Funding CMEP through CFE-DMHA was intended to alleviate these constraints and enable U.S. personnel to work with disaster-management personnel who operate under the ministries of interior or civilian agencies of a partner nation. Yet legal and bureaucratic complications over the transfer of funds, as well as CFE-DMHA's limited administrative capacity, created obstacles in planning for the assumption of responsibility for CMEP.[51] Limited staffing prevented the center from reassigning a government employee to coordinate the CMEP effort and required hiring a contractor who was not capable of performing inherently government functions.[52] A lack of resources and of a financial manager further constrained CFE-DMHA's ability to undertake new tasks.[53] Moreover, PACOM preferred that CFE-DMHA maintain its focus on the Pacific, while both EUCOM and U.S. Central Command (CENTCOM) were concerned with CFE-DMHA's lack of familiarity with their AORs and the expense of personnel traveling from Hawaii to conduct training events.[54] (EUCOM also hesitated to work with CFE-DMHA because of EUCOM's previous experience with CFE-DMHA liaisons and subsequent contract disputes with the center.[55])

In May 2014, Milligan departed CFE-DMHA, and Col Joseph Martin became its interim director. Martin came to the center after serving as the director of PACOM's Pacific Outreach Directorate (J9), as well as in a wide range of command and staff positions in the PACOM AOR. Like his predecessors, Martin began his tenure by reviewing the center's mission, under-

---

[48] Conversation with current or former DoD official and current or former HADR organization staff, 2015.

[49] The CMEP program was initiated by OSD in 1996 to work with former Warsaw Pact nations on emergency-preparedness cooperation. WIF, which provides the CMEP program with $3 million in annual funding, was renamed the Wales Initiative Fund in September 2014 but continues to be referred to as WIF. Chris Prawdzik, "Preparing Partners for Emergencies," *Defense Media Network*, March 14, 2011; and CFE-DMHA, *Command History: January 1–December 31, 2014*, Ford Island, Hawaii, 2015g.

[50] Conversation with current or former DoD official and current or former HADR organization staff, 2015; and conversation with current or former DoD official, 2014.

[51] Conversation with current or former DoD official and current or former HADR organization staff, 2015. OSD lawyers deemed it necessary for CMEP funding to be converted from the WIF's defense-wide O&M account to the Navy's O&M account and then funneled through PACOM. Undertaking such a complex money transfer for a small program was untenable (to the OSD comptroller), and the reprogramming of funds proved impossible because of the center's position as a DRU under PACOM.

[52] Inherently government functions include the management of human resources and policy formation. *Federal Register*, Vol. 76, No. 176, Washington, D.C.: U.S. Government Printing Office, September 12, 2011.

[53] Conversation with current or former DoD official and current or former HADR organization staff, 2015.

[54] Conversation with current or former DoD official and current or former HADR organization staff, 2015; conversation with current or former DoD official, 2014; and CFE-DMHA, 2014b. Ultimately, the complexity involved in transitioning CMEP to CFE-DMHA and the limits placed on executing its unique authority led OSD to ask the Center for Civil-Military Relations (CCMR) to assume responsibility for the program. CCMR, which operated under the Naval Post-Graduate School and served as an interim program manager, appeared to have an organizational and funding structure (as well as a global mandate) that was more suitable to CMEP.

[55] Conversation with current or former DoD official and current or former HADR organization staff, 2015.

taking an extensive strategy-to-task analysis. Martin considered all the previous guidance the center had received (from Title 10 legislation, PACOM MOUs, and OSD memos) and the level of resources the center needed to support each of its activities and missions. He concluded that CFE-DMHA had 70 enduring and 21 implied tasks, and a total of 158 specific required activities. Of these 158 activities, only 44, or 28 percent, were fully resourced, while 74 activities were partially resourced and 40 lacked any support.[56] Based on this review, Martin recommended to PACOM that CFE-DMHA reduce the number of activities in which it engaged, focusing more on education, training, information sharing, and regional engagement in Asia and the Pacific, and less on exercises and PACOM theater-cooperation planning, where he found that the center lacked a comparative advantage.[57]

While undertaking this review, CFE-DMHA continued to engage in a range of education and training activities. It conducted H.E.L.P and HART courses and developed an online HART class. The center continued to engage in information-sharing activities through the publication of *Liaison* and DMHA country assessments, an updated website and virtual-information resource center, and the launching of a social-media campaign in an effort to extend its outreach. It also continued its engagement in CBRN events and to conduct training exercises, workshops, and bilateral engagements, as well as to advise and assist PACOM and regional partners during disasters.[58] CFE-DMHA provided civ-mil coordination during Typhoon Hagupit (Ruby) in the Philippines in December 2014. Most of the its activities under Martin took place within the PACOM AOR.[59] One of its few global efforts, requested by OSD, was to review the curriculum for a peacekeeping course. Another request by OSD was for CFE-DMHA to provide assistance during the Ebola outbreak, but this was declined by the joint force commander and AFRICOM.[60] CFE-DMHA was therefore less active globally in 2014 than it was in 2013.

Charting a Course for the Future

By the end of 2014, CFE-DMHA was pursuing a narrower set of activities, focusing on training and education, information sharing, and regional engagement within the Pacific region.[61] Rather than looking to expand its mission, it made greater effort to further focus its efforts, as the center anticipated further staffing and budget cuts in FYs 2015 and 2016.[62] The center

---

[56] CFE-DMHA, 2014b.

[57] CFE-DMHA, 2014b.

[58] According to its 2014 command history, CFE-DMHA conducted 15 senior-level engagements, 11 engagements with Association of Southeast Asian Nations (ASEAN) organizations and affiliates, 21 training and education courses, and ten formal partnerships. CFE-DMHA, 2015g.

[59] CFE-DMHA, *Deliverables*, briefing, Ford Island, Hawaii, 2012d.

[60] Conversation with current or former CFE-DMHA staff, 2015; conversation with current or former DoD official, 2015; and conversation with current or former DoD official, 2014.

[61] Phone conversation with current or former CFE-DMHA staff, 2014; phone conversation with current or former HADR organization staff, 2015; and CFE-DMHA, 2015g.

[62] The center's staff was expected to decrease to 23 in 2016, with funding reduced to $4 million. Conversation with current or former CFE-DMHA staff, 2015.

therefore sought to emphasize for the future the types of activities it did best and also offered the greatest return on investment.

By spring 2015, CFE-DMHA Director Joe Martin's review of the center had led to a plan for moving it toward more-sustainable and more-effective disaster management efforts within existing budget constraints. The plan, outlined in the center's FY 2016–2020 program plan, involved sharpening CFE-DMHA's focus on the three core lines of effort (training and education, applied research and information sharing, and regional civ-mil coordination) and the three enabling functions (partnering, mission support, and advice and assistance) where the center's capabilities and expertise could be best harnessed.[63] This also meant shedding seven lines of effort that had been only partially resourced and that could be taken up by other organizations, particularly on the PACOM staff. The plan sought to solidify the center's activities in the PACOM AOR in the near term and aspired to an incremental expansion of the three core lines of effort to meet the needs of other CCMDs over the longer term. At the same time, Martin sought to put the center in a better position to pursue these lines of effort through a small increase in USG civilians and associated budget adjustments and through preparations to hire the next director and negotiate a new support contract. Finally, the center undertook a rebranding effort by dropping *HA* from its name (it is now going by *CFE-DM*) and unveiling a new logo that does not depict DoD-related graphics, as seen in the previous one. Notably, Martin developed the center's plan through open consultation with PACOM and OSD leadership to ensure that those who would provide guidance to the CFE-DMHA director (both Martin and future directors) are fully engaged in the process and have the needed insight into the requirements the center seeks to meet. However, it was too early to tell, at the time of writing, how the changes instituted at CFE-DMHA will affect the performance of its missions and the level of internal stability at the center.

Conclusion: A History Marked by Internal Challenges and Successive Reorientation

Since its founding in 1994, CFE-DMHA has undergone significant changes in both its type of activities and its scope, as it has struggled to achieve the objectives of its broad mandate with limited staff and resources. Initially an academically oriented organization with an emphasis on education and research on issues of public health, the center took a more operational focus and became engaged in advising and assisting PACOM in conducting humanitarian assistance operations and training partner nations in terrorist response after 2001. From 2008 to 2012, the center became more closely tied to the military and attempted to develop global risk indicators and engage across the geographic CCMDs. In 2013, CFE-DMHA shifted from having a narrower focus on providing education and training for PACOM to a more global focus on information sharing and collaboration tools. CFE-DMHA also proposed assuming responsibility for the CMEP program. Today, the center is pursuing a narrower set of training and education, information-sharing, and regional engagement activities within the Pacific region, while continuing to debate its future direction.

---

[63] CFE-DMHA, *Meeting Disaster Management Challenges with Excellence: Program Plan FY16–20*, Ford Island, Hawaii, October 1, 2015f, pp. 3–4. See also "CFE-DM Initiatives," Center for Excellence in Disaster Management and Humanitarian Assistance, undated.

These shifts were the result of the personal styles, backgrounds, and priorities of the center's successive directors, as well as changes in the availability of external funding sources. The shifts may also be attributed to a lack of specific guidance from OSD and PACOM to constrain personal choices and adaptation to the requirements of CFE-DMHA's broad mandate with unchanging or even decreasing levels of funding and staff.

As CFE-DMHA has attempted to expand its scope of activities both within and beyond the Asia-Pacific region, there have been a number of unsuccessful attempts to improve CFE-DMHA's organizational structure and to provide the center with additional manpower. Struggles with funding, manpower (particularly government personnel to manage inherently governmental tasks), and organization and oversight to cover a broader range of activities have, at times, threatened the health of the organization. There have also been various proposals to combine the center with other organizations in Hawaii, such as the APCSS and PDC, or national military education organizations, such as the National Defense University. Yet throughout its 22-year history, the center has remained independent and has continued to struggle with internal turmoil in attempting to navigate its broad mandate with limited resources and oversight. These three key issues—internal change and staff turnover, mandate not aligning with resources, and inconsistent oversight—represent endemic problems for the center that continue into the present and need to be addressed. The current director's efforts are aimed at mitigating the challenges that have arisen as a result, but the outcome of these efforts remains to be seen. How has the center performed in the past in light of these challenges? This is the topic of the next chapter.

CHAPTER THREE

A Review and Assessment of the Center's Activities

This chapter assesses the activities CFE-DMHA was undertaking as of 2015—education and training, advise and assist, engagements and exercises, and information sharing[1]—and evaluates its ability to perform these functions with its current resources. The first section uses CFE-DMHA's handful of metrics, as well as documents and interviews, to highlight CFE-DMHA's most-successful activities and potential niches. The second section examines the guidance and funding the center receives, its manpower size and structure, and its mission-support functions to determine what attributes a functioning civ-mil coordination entity such as CFE-DMHA requires to properly fulfill its mandate. Although we obtained a great deal of information from multiple sources, including interviews with CFE-DMHA staff, annual reports, and internal assessment reports, the following discussion is not meant to be a comprehensive evaluation of CFE-DMHA assessment practices. Rather, our goals are to highlight the types of metrics CFE-DMHA is using, to provide an assessment of CFE-DMHA's ability to reach its stated goals through its activities, and to recognize areas of strength and opportunities for further development.

An Assessment of the Center's Activities

CFE-DMHA has a wide range of activities, from advise and assist to information sharing, that result in it organizing or participating in a large number of events—95 per year, on average, from FY 2010 to FY 2012.[2] The center has a number of metrics that can support an evaluation of its activities, some of which we discuss below. Yet, in most cases, as with many other USG organizations, it does not have a proper assessment process to determine the impact of its activities on expected outcomes, making it difficult to evaluate the extent to which it succeeds in fulfilling its mission. CFE-DMHA tracks outputs in many areas but, among outcomes, it systematically evaluates only training and, to a lesser extent, information sharing. This section

---

[1] These categories mirror those used by CFE-DMHA to describe its current activities (see "Strategy to Task Analysis," Center for Excellence in Disaster Management and Humanitarian Assistance, undated).

[2] Specifically, there were 97 events in FY 2010, 104 in FY 2011, and 85 in FY 2012 (COE-DMHA, *COE DMHA Events Fiscal Year 2010*, internal document, Honolulu, undated-c; CFE-DMHA, *FY 2011 Theater Campaign Plan Event Summary, Center for Excellence in Disaster Management and Humanitarian Assistance*, internal document, Ford Island, Hawaii, undated-d; CFE-DMHA, *Center for Excellence in Disaster Management and Humanitarian Assistance (COE-DMHA) FY12 Events*, internal document, Ford Island, Hawaii, undated-a). It is unclear how comprehensive these listings of events are, because the one for FY 2010 does not include a single HART course, while 16 such courses are listed for FY 2011 and 13 for FY 2012.

assesses the main activities of CFE-DMHA using CFE-DMHA metrics where they exist, as well as a large number of interviews conducted by the RAND team with former and current CFE-DMHA staff and other stakeholders. We also suggest in Appendix B additional metrics to develop for measuring organizational effectiveness, while recognizing that any comprehensive and systematic assessment methodology would most likely require resources that CFE-DMHA does not currently have.

Education and Training

Education and training are CFE-DMHA's most thoroughly assessed activities. CFE-DMHA administers daily course critiques and an overall course evaluation to training participants to determine possible areas for improvement. Course managers and partner organizations also conduct qualitative reviews of course curriculum.

Current CFE-DMHA training and education efforts include HART, which is taught both in a classroom setting and online; H.E.L.P.; and Disaster Management and Humanitarian Assistance 101, which provides background knowledge on all aspects of DMHA in the Asia-Pacific.[3] A December 2014 MOU between CFE-DMHA and the United Nations Office for the Coordination of Humanitarian Affairs (OCHA) and a "train the trainer" effort in March 2015 enabled CFE-DMHA to cofacilitate with OCHA instructors the discussions that compose the United Nations Civil-Military Coordination (UN-CMCoord) and Supporting Humanitarian Action in Response to Emergencies and Disasters (SHARED) courses, broadening CFE-DMHA's list of course offerings and reinforcing its relationship with OCHA.[4]

HART

HART is an operational-level course offered in both a classroom setting over three to four days and online via Joint Knowledge Online. HART focuses on a number of key areas of civ-mil coordination—from humanitarian principles to the institutional actors involved in a response—in the context of a humanitarian emergency.[5] While HART's primary audience is military personnel (ranking from senior enlisted to O-5–O-6) assigned to PACOM contingency missions for foreign disaster operations,[6] CFE-DMHA is adapting the course for partner nations (e.g., Canada and Singapore).[7]

HART course participants rate 24 specific items across six major sections: (1) course content, (2) instruction, (3) hands-on application and discussion, (4) course materials, (5) training environment, and (6) length of course. Participants are also asked to recommend specific improvements to the course, as well as additional topics they would like to see addressed in

---

[3]   CFE-DMHA also provides as a resource a list of other training courses available on a variety of DMHA-related issues and provided by various U.S. and international organizations ("Training Courses," Center for Excellence in Disaster Management and Humanitarian Assistance, undated).

[4]   E-mail correspondences with current or former CFE-DMHA staff and current or former HADR organization staff, September 2015.

[5]   "Humanitarian Assistance Response Training (HART) Course," Center for Excellence in Disaster Management and Humanitarian Assistance, undated.

[6]   Conversation with current or former CFE-DMHA staff, 2015; CFE-DMHA, *Information Paper; Subject: Center for Excellence in Disaster Management (CFE-DM) Communication Platforms and Product Metrics from January to July 2015*, Ford Island, Hawaii, August 10, 2015e.

[7]   Conversation with current or former CFE-DMHA staff, 2015; e-mail correspondence with current or former CFE-DMHA staff, 2015.

future CFE-DMHA events. Among the 302 participants in nine classroom HART courses that CFE-DMHA taught from January to July 2015, the average student approval rating was 4.8 on a 5-point scale, on which a 5 indicated the most positive evaluation.[8] Such high ratings do not appear to be exceptional. Students in the 18 classroom HART courses provided from 2010 to 2012 gave the course average ratings of at least 4.5 on the same 5-point scale.[9]

Some discussants flagged some potential similarities between the HART course and the Joint Humanitarian Operations Course (JHOC) offered by USAID and OFDA. In recent years, the HART course has been adapted to emphasize its difference from JHOC. It now focuses more specifically on predeployment training for the U.S. military, teaching participants how to work on HADR missions, how to inform a commander, and how to connect with OFDA. The HART course also focuses more on the international, rather than U.S., dimension of the response, with the objective of making the two courses complementary.[10] Meanwhile, JHOC focuses more specifically on the processes through which OFDA and DoD operate together during a disaster response. One respondent with first-hand knowledge of JHOC stated that "there is a place for both courses" and did not find them to be redundant.[11] OFDA also works with CFE-DMHA on the HART course. In the past, the OFDA lead at PACOM has provided a short presentation of OFDA during the HART course. OFDA has also reviewed some of the HART material upon CFE-DMHA request.[12]

Another interviewee raised a concern about redundancy between HART and UN-CMCoord courses, specifically in their focus on the international dimension of the response.[13] One discussant described HART as "a variation of the UN-CMCoord adapted to a U.S. military audience" but claimed, for that audience, HART works best.[14] Cost considerations, however, led another discussant to claim that while HART is a "well put-together course," depending on their location, participants may find it cheaper to attend the UN-CMCoord course instead. In 2015, for instance, CFE-DMHA taught HART in Hawaii, the continental United States (Washington state and California), and Japan, but that same year UN-CMCoord was taught in Europe (Ireland and Germany), the Middle East (Jordan), Southeast Asia (Malaysia), Africa (Uganda), and the Pacific (Fiji), in addition to Washington, D.C.[15]

---

[8] CFE-DMHA, 2015e.

[9] CFE-DMHA, *H.E.L.P. Course Critique Summary Spreadsheet*, internal document, Ford Island, Hawaii, undated-e.

[10] Conversation with current or former CFE-DMHA staff, 2015; phone conversation with current or former CFE-DMHA staff, 2015; and phone conversation with current or former CFE-DMHA staff, 2015. These discussants viewed positively the HART course and its uniqueness in relation with the JHOC. A fourth discussant suggested that having only the JHOC would suffice (conversation with current or former PACOM officials, 2015).

[11] Phone conversation with current or former HADR organization staff, 2015.

[12] Phone conversation with current or former HADR organization staff, 2015.

[13] Phone conversation with current or former CFE-DMHA staff, 2015.

[14] Phone conversation with current or former CFE-DMHA staff, 2015.

[15] Phone conversation with current or former CFE-DMHA staff, 2015; email correspondence with CFE-DMHA staff, September 2015; and OCHA, "UN-CMCoord Training and Partnership Programme, Calendar of Events, 2015," 2015. These locations only include the UN-CMCoord course. They do not include UN-CMCoord field courses, global UN-CMCoord skills workshops, the SHARED course, or the Training of Trainers course.

The classroom HART course takes place approximately 12 times a year,[16] while the HART online course is taken, on average, 67 times monthly.[17] Classroom HART courses are full without advertising.[18] This suggests that CFE-DMHA addresses an important need and could serve more if it expanded. One discussant suggested that CFE-DMHA offer a follow-on course to HART, who called it a "great intro course" but regretted that there was not more to it.[19]

H.E.L.P.

The H.E.L.P. course was developed in 1986 by the International Committee of the Red Cross (ICRC) to teach practitioners about public-health issues arising in the context of a humanitarian emergency.[20] CFE-DMHA is accredited by the ICRC to teach the course, which the center offers once yearly in Hawaii. The only other U.S. institution to teach this course is Johns Hopkins University. CFE-DMHA is the only military organization in the world to offer the H.E.L.P. course.[21] The audience for the course is Asia-Pacific military and civilians, as well as the U.S. military.

The course has seen changes in enrollment and funding in recent years. The number of students for the course, which exceeded 50 in 2013, decreased sharply to 20 in 2015, as the result of a change in DoD policy that eliminated scholarships.[22] Participants are asked to rate specific components of the course, using 22 items similar to those for the HART course. Such components include facilities and services (e.g., classroom conditions and food and beverage), instructor quality (e.g., presenters set a positive example of military bearing), course materials (e.g., the course syllabus was useful), and length and pace of the training program. Participants also provided an overall evaluation of the course, giving it an average rating of 4.53 on a 5-point scale (with 5 being excellent).[23]

Metrics for the HART or the H.E.L.P. courses that measure how much participants learn would be useful. Box 3.1 outlines some potential metrics that CFE-DMHA may want to consider for assessing its training activities.

Advise-and-Assist DoD Components

Advise-and-assist activities consist of CFE-DMHA providing DMHA subject-matter expertise to DoD components, primarily PACOM, to help develop programs, plan operations, and design and execute exercises. In 2013, the PACOM commander designated CFE-DMHA as the DMHA coordinating authority for PACOM: "As coordinating authority, CFE will advise USPACOM on DMHA operations, actions, and activities (OAA) and engage with foreign

---

[16] This number varied over the years—for instance, there were 16 courses in 2011 (CFE-DMHA, undated-d).

[17] CFE-DMHA, 2015e.

[18] Conversation with current or former CFE-DMHA staff, 2015.

[19] Phone conversation with current or former EUCOM staff, 2015.

[20] "Health Emergencies in Large Populations (H.E.L.P.) Course," Center for Excellence in Disaster Management and Humanitarian Assistance, undated.

[21] Conversation with current or former CFE-DMHA staff, 2015; conversation with current or former CFE-DMHA staff, 2015.

[22] Conversation with current or former CFE-DMHA staff, 2015.

[23] CFE-DMHA, undated-e.

Box 3.1. How Can CFE-DMHA's Assessment of Its Training Education and Activities Improve?

Although course critiques are useful for monitoring short-term outcomes of training and education programs, training evaluations should also address other outcomes targeted by the training program, including changes in knowledge or perceptions. Evaluations could include factual questions rather than simply personal opinions. For example, an evaluation of knowledge gained from participating in the HART course may include the extent to which training participants can identify specific humanitarian-agency areas of expertise and mechanisms to use for coordinating a response to a disaster. An ideal method for evaluating knowledge gains would be to use a pre-test and post-test research design, assessing participants' knowledge at the start and conclusion of the course. However, training participants can sometimes react negatively to assessment of knowledge.

More-advanced training evaluation designs should be considered for evaluating the achievement of long-term outcomes (e.g., changes in participant behavior). To evaluate intermediate outcomes, course managers should coordinate with a program-evaluation specialist to discuss how to gather the right data. Data-collection methods may include a combination of interviews, focus groups, or surveys to gather feedback about how participants have applied the training they received.

partners on the same."[24] CFE-DMHA also provides disaster-response advice and assistance to PACOM and helps coordinate PACOM events with foreign partners and regional DMHA organizations, such as PACOM visits to the Singapore Regional Coordination Center.[25]

No metrics exist to measure progress on these activities. According to one discussant, potential indicators of success would be increased numbers of requests for CFE-DMHA SMEs, or numbers of former CFE-DMHA liaisons and experts who are hired by CCMDs (e.g., a EUCOM liaison hired by EUCOM).[26] The research team had to rely on anecdotal evidence to assess the quality of CFE-DMHA efforts here. One discussant judged that CFE-DMHA "provided top-level policy and strategic advice."[27] Another noted that CFE-DMHA has great potential to bring significant country knowledge to feed J3's operational missions—a role that CFE-DMHA already fulfills to some extent through its country books (see below) but that used to be more prominent in the mid-2000s.[28] To some extent, CFE-DMHA's advise-and-assist role is redundant with that of OFDA, the lead humanitarian advisor to PACOM. In the past, both organizations have been largely on the same page when it comes to pro-

[24] PACOM, "Decision Memo; Subject: (U) CFE-DMHA Designation as Disaster Management and Humanitarian Assistance Coordinating Authority for U.S. Pacific Command," October 24, 2013.

[25] Conversation with current or former PACOM officials, 2015.

[26] Conversation with current or former DoD official, 2015.

[27] Email follow-up to phone conversation with current or former DoD official, 2015.

[28] Conversation with current or former PACOM officials, 2015.

viding PACOM with advice,[29] suggesting that the potential for conflict is limited. Interestingly, several discussants suggested that CFE-DMHA should help coordinate all PACOM DMHA components—a role it has but for which it is evidently not recognized. One discussant stated that CFE-DMHA could facilitate coordination between the components and the PACOM staff directorates if CFE-DMHA were resourced properly and had the authority to do it, adding: "If CFE was empowered to have a coordinating ability, that would be ideal."[30]

Engagements and Exercises

Engagements encompass all CFE-DMHA activities with non-DoD components, including partnerships with such organizations as the Association of Southeast Asian Nations (ASEAN); international and interagency coordination; and support to bilateral, trilateral, and multilateral defense dialogues.[31] The logic or theory behind such engagements is that increased collaboration will strengthen important relationships necessary to respond efficiently and effectively when a disaster strikes. Interaction with ASEAN has been growing through CFE-DMHA involvement in such forums as the ASEAN Defense Ministers Meetings–Plus Expert Working Group and the ASEAN Regional Forum.[32]

CFE-DMHA's engagement activities may include working-group meetings, conferences, and disaster-planning exercises. Although CFE-DMHA tracks these events by location, date, and duration, it does not assess their impact. To be sure, this is a complex topic to assess. It would be difficult to attribute improvement in a partner's government response to disasters to CFE-DMHA's engagement activities. One discussant did claim that foreign-government agencies "have made their own strides over time."[33] Another noted that, for workshops seeking to help agencies coordinate their responses to emergencies, a potential metric would be, after the event, asking at various intervals (e.g., six months, one year, and three years after the event) how many times the participants had meetings with other agencies.[34]

Several discussants claimed that CFE-DMHA has a comparative advantage in engagement activities for a number of reasons. First, its special authority allowing use of Title 10 funds to engage not just foreign military but also civilians from other ministries gives it a unique and frequent opportunity to support civ-mil engagement.[35] This enables CFE-DMHA to have all-inclusive activities in foreign countries, a point that is particularly important for disaster preparedness, which cannot rely only on the military.[36] Second, CFE-DMHA has developed networks and relationships within partner nations, especially in disaster-management orga-

---

[29] Phone conversation with current or former HADR organization staff, 2015.

[30] Phone conversation with current or former OSD official, 2015.

[31] "Strategy to Task Analysis," undated.

[32] Conversation with current or former DoD officials, 2015; conversation with current or former CFE-DMHA staff, 2015.

[33] Conversation with current or former PACOM officials, 2015.

[34] Phone conversation with current or former HADR organization staff, 2015. This discussant added that if there were zero or one such meetings, then CFE-DMHA would know that it did not changed the system.

[35] Conversation with current or former DoD official, 2014.

[36] Conversation with current or former DoD official, 2014.

nizations.[37] Third, CFE-DMHA's staff is relatively stable compared with PACOM's[38]—an important comparative advantage for CFE-DMHA considering the importance of "face time" and long-term relationships for engagement activities.[39] In sum, CFE-DMHA has the ability to act as a bridge between civilian and military organizations, as demonstrated by its collaboration with OCHA, as well as the World Food Program and other organizations.[40] CFE-DMHA was described as being able to "go places where the military is not welcome"—a clear asset for PACOM and components.[41] One illustration of CFE-DMHA's value in this regard is its participation in a nascent trilateral model of engagement involving Burma, Thailand, and the United States. In 2013, CFE-DMHA helped shape a workshop on military medicine and DMHA that included both Thailand and Burma, with Thailand facilitating Burma's participation.[42]

Interviewees highlighted several other CFE-DMHA initiatives. One receiving positive reviews is the role played by CFE-DMHA in helping Thailand develop its Civil-Military Guidelines for Disaster Management in cooperation with the Joint U.S. Military Advisory Group Thailand (JUSMAGTHAI).[43] One indicator of success for this initiative is that the guidelines have been implemented across military and civilian agencies in Thailand.[44] Another initiative of note is the development of five-year DMHA engagement country plans for Mongolia, Fiji, and Nepal, which compiled and analyzed country strategies from the State Department and USAID, the Theater Security Cooperation Plan, and international organizations to recommend successive engagement steps with Nepal. One discussant described this activity as "very valuable."[45] Finally, CFE-DMHA, in 2015, began to conduct country gap assessments using a method developed by the Defense Threat Reduction Agency (DTRA) and West Point and adapted by CFE-DMHA to disaster management.[46] These assessments reportedly provide DoD and U.S. embassies in the PACOM AOR with a clear perspective on partner nations' key gaps, as well as a plan for U.S. engagement to fill these gaps.[47] CFE-DMHA sent a package of country-specific documents providing a very preliminary assessment to the U.S. Office of Defense Cooperation and the ambassadors in the Philippines, Bangladesh, and Mongolia and

---

[37] Phone conversation with current or former DoD official, 2015.

[38] It must be acknowledged, however, that some civilian staff at PACOM have a longevity similar to CFE-DMHA's staff.

[39] Conversation with current or former PACOM officials, 2015.

[40] Phone conversation with current or former CFE-DMHA staff, 2014; conversation with current or former CFE-DMHA staff, 2015.

[41] Conversation with current or former CFE-DMHA staff, 2015.

[42] Phone conversation with current or former DoD official, 2015.

[43] Email follow-up to phone conversation with current or former DoD official, 2015.

[44] Phone conversation with current or former DoD official, 2015.

[45] Conversation with current or former PACOM official, 2015.

[46] Conversation with current or former CFE-DMHA staff, 2015.

[47] "CFE-DMHA, *Subject: Disaster Management Country Assessment Program*, information paper, internal document, Ford Island, Hawaii, June 18, 2015c.

offered to conduct a full assessment.[48] In response, the U.S. ambassador to Bangladesh invited CFE-DMHA to participate in a disaster-response exercise and exchange in September 2015.[49]

Another area where CFE-DMHA supports PACOM is the planning and conduct of DMHA exercises. CFE-DMHA has been involved, for instance, in Balikatan with the Philippines and Cobra Gold with Thailand, among others. As of summer 2015, CFE-DMHA was planning to develop a curriculum for the senior leaders' seminar held at the start of PACOM exercises with foreign governments.[50] We could not assess the effectiveness of CFE-DMHA's support to exercises. Nevertheless, it is unclear what unique value CFE-DMHA brings to these exercises. One discussant complained that CFE-DMHA supports exercises merely by augmenting the staff of the PACOM J7.[51] A more useful role for CFE-DMHA in exercises would be in the furtherance of its core civ-mil missions to assess partner-nation DMHA capacity; capture best practices; and coordinate with partner nations, international organizations, and NGOs.[52]

Information Sharing

CFE-DMHA's involvement in information sharing takes different forms: It collects lessons learned from various disaster responses; it serves as a centralized repository for information about disaster- and humanitarian-management documents; and it produces its own materials, including Disaster Management Reference Handbooks, which provide important information about countries most at risk to environmental disasters. CFE-DMHA documents these outputs, as well as several measures of performance related to CFE-DMHA's website,[53] but the center has not developed ways to assess the impact of its information-sharing activities. As a result, we rely on anecdotal evidence gathered through interviews to assess CFE-DMHA's efforts to disseminate knowledge and information about DMHA.

CFE-DMHA Centralizes and Disseminates DMHA Knowledge

A very specific initiative of CFE-DMHA is to systematically collect "lessons observed during response to large-scale disasters and humanitarian emergencies around the globe."[54] This activity is an integral part of Inouye's original idea that the center serve as a repository for lessons learned and best practices.[55] Although the center has collected lessons learned on several large-scale disasters in the Asia-Pacific region, including flooding in Pakistan in 2010, the Japanese earthquake and tsunami in 2011, and the earthquake in Nepal in 2015, it is unclear whether

---

[48] Conversation with current or former CFE-DMHA staff, 2015; email correspondence with current or former CFE-DMHA staff, 2015.

[49] Email correspondence with current or former CFE-DMHA staff, 2015.

[50] Conversation with current or former CFE-DMHA staff, 2015.

[51] Conversation with current or former CFE-DMHA staff, 2015.

[52] Comment from DoD officials, March 16, 2016.

[53] CFE-DMHA tracks number of sessions, page views, and unique users; average session time; provenance of users (the United States or rest of the world); popular pages; and product downloads (CFE-DMHA, *CFE-DMHA Web Presence, Measures of Performance*, briefing, internal document, Ford Island, Hawaii, January 2015a).

[54] "Lessons Learned," Center for Excellence in Disaster Management and Humanitarian Assistance, undated.

[55] Conversation with current or former DoD official, 2014.

its efforts here can be considered systematic.[56] CFE-DMHA's repository of lessons learned is available through its Virtual Information Resource Center, an online library with more than a thousand entries for documents—including after-action reports, best practices, and assessments—related to disaster management.

CFE-DMHA also plays an important role in sharing information with military planners at PACOM and civilian organizations in times of crisis. Until 2010, it issued regular reports on humanitarian emergencies (humanitarian crisis reports). It also published crisis reports specific to various areas, such as the Asia-Pacific region (Asia-Pacific Daily Reports), Afghanistan (Afghanistan Humanitarian Assistance Reports), and Iraq (Iraq Humanitarian Assistance Reports). The purpose of these various reports was to track the major actions taken by parties responding to the crisis.[57] CFE-DMHA also published a weekly disease-surveillance report (Asia-Pacific Disease Outbreak/Surveillance Report). These reports came to a halt in 2009 (for the Asia-Pacific Daily Reports) and 2010 (for the three others).[58]

Since 2010, CFE-DMHA has typically prepared daily CFE-DMHA disaster-information reports—including those on the 2011 Japan tsunami, Typhoon Hagupit in the Philippines, and the 2015 Nepal earthquake—if there is interest from PACOM.[59] In early 2015, for instance, CFE-DMHA issued a CFE-DMHA Humanitarian Information Paper (CHIP) outlining key concerns and trends, as well as background information, on the Rohingya migration crisis in Burma. CHIP documents start with a "BLUF [bottom line up front]—Potential Implications to PACOM" box—evidence that PACOM remains the main customer for CFE-DMHA's crisis-information products.[60] In contrast to other similar products, such as the crisis reports issued by the United Nations' ReliefWeb, CFE-DMHA reports are designed to inform the PACOM commander rather than the entire DMHA community—a practice that, according to one discussant, started under the leadership of Goodman.[61]

CFE-DMHA's comparative advantage in this area lies in its relationships with other stakeholders (particularly civilians) to get information about what is happening on the ground and its use of both military and nonmilitary sources, which enhances the credibility of its information.[62] CFE-DMHA serves as a relay between the U.S. military and civilian organizations, sending information to, for instance, OCHA. One discussant described CFE-DMHA's work here as "extremely useful."[63] During crises, CFE-DMHA provides reports on what all actors are doing, using its contacts with civilian organizations, such as OCHA, ASEAN's Coordinating Centre for Humanitarian Assistance Center, or the Changi Regional HADR Coordination Centre in Singapore. Through CFE-DMHA, PACOM J3 also shares with these organizations

---

[56] Conversation with current or former PACOM official, 2015.

[57] The frequency of these reports has decreased to weekly rather than daily (email correspondence with current or former CFE-DMHA staff, 2015).

[58] Email correspondence with current or former CFE-DMHA staff, 2015.

[59] Email correspondence with current or former CFE-DMHA staff, 2015.

[60] CFE-DMHA, *Rohingya Crisis*, Ford Island, Hawaii, Humanitarian Information Paper No. 1, May 22, 2015b.

[61] Conversation with current or former CFE-DMHA staff, 2015.

[62] Conversation with current or former CFE-DMHA staff, 2015; conversation with current or former CFE-DMHA staff, 2015.

[63] Phone conversation with current or former HADR organization staff, 2015.

what PACOM is doing.[64] Hence, CFE-DMHA is considered to provide "a broader picture" than other organizations do.[65]

CFE-DMHA also relays various sources of information about current crises through its Twitter account. The center provides links to OCHA's Disaster Information Reports as they appear. Some of this activity overlaps with much more widely accessed crisis-response systems of PDC, such as its DisasterAWARE platform, which monitors and maps areas at risk of experiencing a disaster. The two organizations are planning to collaborate in this domain, discussing in 2015 the possibility of linking CFE-DMHA products in DisasterAWARE.[66] Finally, since 1999, CFE-DMHA has published *Liaison*, a journal on DMHA issues. The stated purpose of the journal is to "promote the ability of DMHA partners to learn from one another through lessons learned to build a stronger DMHA community through shared learning."[67] One discussant noted that contributions were, at least initially, "mediocre."[68] Although this discussant claimed the quality of the articles has since improved, the discussant still questioned whether the articles have the depth that one would expect in such a journal.[69] *Liaison* is now online and published biannually.[70]

CFE-DMHA Produces DMHA Knowledge

Beyond gathering after-action reports and best practices from other organizations, CFE-DMHA also collects its own information about lessons learned and best practices. The demand for such information comes from both military and civilians (CCMDs, national-disaster management organizations, international organizations, and NGOs).[71] In 2013, CFE-DMHA sent a team to the Philippines during Typhoon Haiyan to collect lessons learned. Although its initial draft report was considered unsatisfactory,[72] the report was subsequently revised and disseminated to good reviews.[73] One discussant noted that "CFE's biggest demand" is to capture lessons learned and best practices and discuss how to apply and operationalize them.[74] Another noted the high frequency at which CFE-DMHA is asked, during events, about lessons learned.[75]

---

[64] Conversation with current or former PACOM officials, 2015.

[65] Phone conversation with current or former HADR organization staff, 2015.

[66] Conversation with current or former HADR organization staff, 2015.

[67] Phone conversation with current or former CFE-DMHA staff, 2015; "Liaison," Center for Excellence in Disaster Management and Humanitarian Assistance, undated.

[68] Phone conversation with current or former CFE-DMHA staff, 2015.

[69] Phone conversation with current or former CFE-DMHA staff, 2015.

[70] Phone conversation with current or former CFE-DMHA staff, 2015.

[71] Conversation with current or former CFE-DMHA staff, 2015.

[72] Phone conversation with current or former CFE-DMHA staff, 2015; conversation with current or former PACOM officials, 2015; phone conversation with current or former CFE-DMHA staff, 2015. Reasons for dissatisfaction with the first draft included possible lack of experience of the CFE-DMHA team with the military perspective and a lack of guidance (phone conversation with current or former CFE-DMHA staff, 2015). The draft also had to be produced very quickly, which may explain its poor quality (phone conversation with current or former CFE-DMHA staff, 2015).

[73] Phone conversation with current or former CFE-DMHA staff, 2015; conversation with current or former DoD official, 2014; conversation with current or former PACOM officials, 2015.

[74] Conversation with current or former CFE-DMHA staff, 2015.

[75] Conversation with current or former CFE-DMHA staff, 2015.

Although CFE-DMHA is but one organization that collects lessons learned, it is well positioned to fill that role. First, CFE-DMHA can take a cross-components and cross-agency view for the benefit of DoD.[76] Second, its relatively stable staff (when compared with the PACOM and PACOM components' staff) provides some degree of continuity and learning over time. Finally, because CFE-DMHA produces unclassified lessons, they can be shared with U.S. partners.[77] CFE-DMHA's other activities also suggest possible synergies; the center could use these lessons learned, for example, to inform its own training activities.[78] Similarly, lessons learned can be incorporated into CFE-DMHA's research activities (see below).

CFE-DMHA also produces Disaster Management Reference Handbooks, which provide a baseline of DMHA capabilities, assets, and actors in partner nations. These handbooks provide background to practitioners about how partner nations are preparing for disasters. As of 2015, books were available on 11 countries—all of which are in the PACOM AOR.[79] The books are updated every three to four years and can be downloaded from the CFE-DMHA website. The number of downloads is the only metric that CFE-DMHA has for interest in the books.[80] In January 2015, seven of the ten most downloaded CFE-DMHA products were country handbooks.[81] To put these books together, CFE-DMHA coordinates with country teams, OFDA, and OCHA for review and input.[82] CFE-DMHA also gets feedback from the components.[83]

CFE-DMHA's handbooks were described by various discussants as making "a lot of sense" and being "useful,"[84] "excellent,"[85] "long needed,"[86] "a good product,"[87] and "indispensable" to PACOM in developing five-year strategies based on partner needs and helping PACOM task components.[88] One discussant noted that there is no other place to find that information—OFDA may be able to provide some, but not all, of it and not for every country.[89] A more similar endeavor may be PDC's baseline assessments of disaster-management capacities of countries in the U.S. Southern Command (SOUTHCOM) AOR, which are done

[76] Conversation with current or former CFE-DMHA staff, 2015.

[77] Conversation with current or former PACOM officials, 2015.

[78] Conversation with current or former DoD officials, 2015.

[79] The countries are Bangladesh, Burma, Cambodia, Indonesia, Lao PDR, Mongolia, Nepal, Philippines, Sri Lanka, Thailand, and Vietnam ("Disaster Management Reference Handbooks," Center for Excellence in Disaster Management and Humanitarian Assistance, undated).

[80] Conversation with current or former CFE-DMHA staff, 2015. This is a very imperfect metric, because the handbooks can be downloaded from other websites as well. In January 2015, the handbook on the Philippines was the most often downloaded CFE-DMHA product for that month, with 25 downloads ("CFE-DMHA Web Presence, Measures of Performance," briefing, internal document, January 2015).

[81] CFE-DMHA, 2015a.

[82] Conversation with current or former CFE-DMHA staff, 2015.

[83] Conversation with current or former PACOM officials, 2015.

[84] Conversation with current or former PACOM officials, 2015.

[85] Phone conversation with current or former HADR organization staff, 2015.

[86] Phone conversation with current or former AFRICOM official, 2015.

[87] Phone conversation with current or former HADR organization staff, 2015.

[88] Conversation with current or former PACOM official, 2015.

[89] Phone conversation with current or former AFRICOM official, 2015.

through on-the-ground data collection by PDC—but, as indicated, they do not cover the Asia-Pacific region.[90]

A few discussants were less enthusiastic about the handbooks. One noted that the country was not the best level of analysis for such handbooks, since there can be considerable variations in disaster-response capacity from region to region or province to province. The same discussant added that a national-level analysis only makes sense for small island states, and that some of the information was not up-to-date.[91] Another discussant argued that CFE-DMHA's handbooks (which average about 140 pages) are too long for operators. This discussant also underlined the difficulty of keeping the information up-to-date, given legislative changes.[92]

Finally, CFE-DMHA has developed a research activity. One example of this capacity is the white paper that CFE-DMHA, in collaboration with PACOM J9, produced in less than one month on the potential impact of El Niño on the PACOM AOR. The paper was said to have attracted the attention of the PACOM commander, because it provided useful findings on where DMHA emergencies may occur in the near future.[93]

One discussant mentioned such "deep dives" as a "niche area that CFE excels at."[94] Other interviewees noted that CFE-DMHA is uniquely placed to link climate change and national security.[95] This is, to some extent, reconnecting with the vision for the center of its first director—that of an academic center of excellence, focused on education, training, and research (see Chapter Two). Since its inception, CFE-DMHA has been partnering with academic institutions—including, as of 2015, the Harvard Humanitarian Initiative, the National Disaster Preparedness Training Center at the University of Hawaii, the University of Hawaii's Office of Public Health Studies, and the Naval Postgraduate School.[96] One discussant noted, however, that reciprocity in that collaboration was sometimes difficult to achieve, given meager CFE-DMHA resources and the notion that CFE-DMHA activities are mainly geared toward PACOM, which might not be of interest to CFE-DMHA's academic partners.[97]

Conclusion: Which Activities Should CFE-DMHA Prioritize?

Given current funding trends, CFE-DMHA needs to either be entirely reimagined (see Chapter Four) or focus on fewer activities and become excellent at those (a focus of its current director), since its level of resources does not allow it to satisfy its giant mandate.[98] If CFE-DMHA chooses the latter option, it should select activities based on three considerations: What does CFE-DMHA do best? For what activities is it uniquely positioned? And what activities can be done through collaboration with other entities?

[90] Conversation with current or former HADR organization staff, 2015; "Disaster Management Agencies Sign Bilateral Agreements," Pacific Disaster Center, July 25, 2014.

[91] Conversation with current or former HADR organization staff, 2015.

[92] Phone conversation with current or former HADR organization staff, 2015.

[93] Conversation with current or former PACOM official, 2015.

[94] Conversation with current or former PACOM official, 2015.

[95] Conversation with current or former CFE-DMHA staff, 2015.

[96] "DMHA Partners," Center for Excellence in Disaster Management and Humanitarian Assistance, undated.

[97] Conversation with current or former CFE-DMHA staff, 2015.

[98] Phone conversation with current or former HADR organization staff, 2015.

CFE-DMHA stakeholders did not identify a consistent set of "niche activities" for the center. One discussant mentioned acting as an interface between the private sector and international organizations on one side and PACOM and components on the other, as well as providing information and engaging people in exercises.[99] Another mentioned that CFE-DMHA had comparative advantages at developing operational concepts on DMHA methods and synthesizing best practices, educating across all pillars of DMHA and to varied types of organizations, medical engagement and capacity-building programs, and maintaining relationships with major NGOs internationally.[100]

Our assessment indicates that training—of U.S. and foreign civilians and military personnel—is an activity where CFE-DMHA adds particular value. Internal CFE-DMHA summary reports compiled from course critiques indicate very high satisfaction among participants for the HART and H.E.L.P. courses. OCHA trusts CFE-DMHA enough to accredit it to cofacilitate the UN-CMCoord course. CFE-DMHA's HART course is different enough from JHOC and UN-CMCoord to create unique value.

Engagement with non-USG organizations is another area where CFE-DMHA brings unique value, because of its ability to show a mostly "civilian face" in spite of being a DoD organization (and in spite of having many staff with a military background). Thanks to its Title 10 authority, for example, it can engage a variety of partners, as it does when including civilians from nonmilitary ministries in its efforts. This allows it to include countries and organizations that are usually reluctant to associate themselves with the U.S. military. Yet CFE-DMHA will never have the capacity to engage everyone everywhere. It should therefore focus on the forums where it has unique access—ASEAN, NGOs—and limit its other engagement activities to a small set of countries of highest priority to OSD and the PACOM[101] commander that could be identified each year, perhaps with flexibility through reprioritization actions that would require removing an engagement activity for each one that is added. The priority for CFE-DMHA's engagement activities should be to prevent mission creep, and this can be done through rigorous strategic planning.

CFE-DMHA's participation in exercises is difficult to assess, but these activities appear to be in support of PACOM J7 in a way that makes CFE-DMHA a surge capacity for J7, rather than an entity that provides unique value. In this sense, exercises may not be where CFE-DMHA's support is most useful.

Information sharing (including research) is an important part of CFE-DMHA's activities. The collection of lessons learned and the country handbooks have received mixed reviews, but they seem to have improved in recent years. It was beyond the scope of this study to examine to what extent CFE-DMHA's crisis information reports are similar to or different from ReliefWeb and other potential competitors. Nevertheless, CFE-DMHA's extensive networks, within both the civilian and military spheres, clearly give it a unique vantage point—and unique access to a variety of information. Information sharing is also the core of what a center of excellence should be doing—collecting and transmitting information about best practices.

The value of *Liaison*, however, remains unclear. Its purpose at the beginning of CFE-DMHA was to connect the various CFE-DMHA's stakeholders, both military and civilians,

---

[99] Phone conversation with current or former HADR organization staff, 2015.

[100] Conversation with current or former CFE-DMHA staff, 2015.

[101] Or other CCMD, if CFE-DMHA were to become a global organization (see Chapter Four).

but this role might now be better fulfilled through CFE-DMHA's website and Twitter account, which advertise CFE-DMHA's and other organizations' research and products to a wider audience than does *Liaison*.

With the main characteristic of a center of excellence being first and foremost its expertise, advise-and-assist functions are also at the core of what CFE-DMHA should be doing, but selectively.[102] It should provide specific functional and regional knowledge to DoD components (including to joint task forces during crises). CFE-DMHA also fulfills a unique role because it was named DMHA coordinator for PACOM in 2013. Hence, even though the center's performance in these activities is difficult to assess, it seems that advise-and-assist activities should remain part of CFE-DMHA's mandate. Yet such activities could be limited in scope to lighten the burden on CFE-DMHA, barring additional funds. For instance, it could be limited to direct advice to OSD, as well as the PACOM[103] commander and the core leadership team, rather than be an equivalent of additional staff for PACOM's planning activities.

Overall, this report's conclusions on activities align with the presently emerging CFE-DMHA focus on training, information sharing, and regional engagement as CFE-DMHA's strongest suits and probably its most important activities. They take advantage of CFE-DMHA's existing networks, its ability to engage a variety of individuals and organizations, and its experience in providing training. In these three areas, CFE-DMHA has developed unique capabilities. It also has a demand signal and support beyond PACOM (to other U.S. and foreign customers). Advise and assist is a set of activities where CFE-DMHA holds unique knowledge that PACOM and other DoD components need. This unique knowledge is also what can help make CFE-DMHA a center of excellence. Therefore, CFE-DMHA should probably not abandon its advise-and-assist activities, which could be added to the three training classes, information sharing, and regional engagement but would most certainly require additional resources. In these four areas, however, CFE-DMHA should focus on those activities for which it brings the most value and which represent the highest priorities for its key stakeholders.

Are the Center's Resources Adequate for Its Mission?

A discussant noted that "four directors in three years [including Goodman] has kind of become the bumper sticker for the CFE."[104] Almost all CFE-DMHA directors left their position under troubling circumstances, suggesting a systemic, rather than an individual or organizational

---

[102] See, for instance, definitions by the Army ("an organization that creates the highest standards of achievement in an assigned sphere of expertise by generating synergy through effective and efficient combination and integration of functions while reinforcing unique requirements and capabilities") and by Carnegie Mellon University, based on a TRADOC definition ("a center of excellence is a premier organization providing an exceptional product or service in an assigned sphere of expertise and within a specific field of technology, business, or government, consistent with the unique requirements and capabilities of the COE organization"). See "Information Papers: Institutional Training Under Centers of Excellence," U.S. Army website, undated; William Craig, Matthew Fisher, Suzanne Garcia-Miller, Clay Kaylor, and John Porter, *Generalized Criteria and Evaluation Method for Center of Excellence: A Preliminary Report*, Pittsburgh, Pa.: Carnegie Mellon University, December 2009.

[103] Or other CCMD, if CFE-DMHA were to become a global organization (see Chapter Four).

[104] Conversation with current or former DoD official, 2014.

problem.[105] This warrants an examination of the conditions under which CFE-DMHA directors pursue their mandate and accomplish their missions. This section first examines the guidance that CFE-DMHA receives from both PACOM and OSD and asks whether this guidance is sufficient to help CFE-DMHA direct its action in ways that make it useful to its stakeholders. Second, it highlights the challenges that CFE-DMHA has encountered with funding. Third, it looks at CFE-DMHA's workforce to identify potential weaknesses that may impede the center's ability to pursue its mission and establish "excellence" in DMHA. Fourth, it examines whether the center has the mission-support functions that it needs to operate.

Guidance

CFE-DMHA's chain of command is a complex one. As a DRU to PACOM, CFE-DMHA is directly subordinate to the PACOM commander. At the same time, an April 24, 2000, message from the Secretary of Defense directs the ASD/SOLIC "to exercise authority, direction, and control over CFE-DMHA through the Director, Joint Staff and USPACOM."[106] This dual authority over CFE-DMHA may create confusion as to who exactly is in charge of steering CFE-DMHA in the right direction and supervising its activities. OSD provides strategic guidance for CFE-DMHA but through PACOM. PACOM supports CFE-DMHA in all other regards. One discussant described this division of labor as OSD being the "51 percent stakeholder," while PACOM is in charge of the "care and feeding."[107]

To some extent, OSD has exercised its role as the provider of strategic guidance for CFE-DMHA, albeit only recently. An October 18, 2013, memo from OSD requests the PACOM commander to "direct CFE to conduct activities in accordance with the following guidance."[108] This guidance outlined the types of activities the center should be pursuing: education and training, advise and assist DoD component staffs, develop partnerships, research, and information sharing. The list of areas to cover is more restricted than in Title 10, Section 182 (there is no specific mention of CBRN or tropical medicine, for instance), and the mission of the center as a "repository of disaster risk indicators for the Asia-Pacific Region" is not mentioned either.[109] Otherwise, the areas specified are still very broad (especially since the memo also mentions CFE-DMHA participating in "USPACOM-directed activities and programs"), and the only point of note in the memo is the mention of the future integration of CMEP into CFE-DMHA.[110] Individuals interviewed for this study described the memo as "vanilla," too

---

[105] The circumstances are related to the internal administrative turmoil mentioned in Chapter Two. This report does not address the details of these circumstances.

[106] Cited in PACOM and CFE-DMHA, "Memorandum of Understanding Between Commander, United States Pacific Command and Director, Center for Excellence in Disaster Management and Humanitarian Assistance," August 24, 2011.

[107] Conversation with current or former PACOM official, 2015.

[108] ASD/SOLIC, 2013.

[109] Title 10, Section 182, is discussed in detail in Chapter Five.

[110] ASD/SOLIC, 2013. An earlier policy memo from Undersecretary of Defense for Policy encouraged the various CCMDs beyond PACOM to take advantage of CFE-DMHA expertise and outlined specific ways in which it can support their respective security cooperation efforts ("USD Policy Memo on Mission of the CFE-DMHA," in "Strategy to Task Analysis," undated).

broad, not offering a vision for CFE-DMHA, and failing to answer the key question of CFE-DMHA's task prioritization based on its limited resources.[111]

CFE-DMHA has received more-frequent guidance from PACOM. This includes:

- the MOU signed annually since 2011 between PACOM and CFE-DMHA "to define the relationship between both parties and to capture the unique arrangements established for the actual provision of administrative support services by USPACOM"[112]
- the October 24, 2013, PACOM commander decision memo that designates CFE-DMHA as the DMHA coordinating authority for PACOM and outlines the center's primary responsibilities along two main lines: coordination of DMHA events with foreign partners, particularly ASEAN, and support to other PACOM staff directorates on DMHA matters[113]
- PACOM Instruction 0530.1, *Command Relationships*.[114]

One discussant also mentioned "intuitive guidance" after reading the commander's priorities.[115] The CFE-DMHA director meets regularly with the PACOM commander's chief of staff, which does not constitute written guidance but can contribute to setting directions for CFE-DMHA on a short-term basis. In contrast, meetings with OSD leadership have been less frequent. Being located in Hawaii, so close to PACOM, also facilitates such interactions, in contrast with the geographical distance that separates CFE-DMHA from OSD.

Although the MOU's Operational Support Annex attempts to clarify the division of roles between CFE-DMHA and different parts of PACOM, and the 2013 PACOM commander's decision memo regarding DMHA coordination provides additional indications as to how CFE-DMHA should support the various PACOM directorates, several individuals interviewed for this study noted that in practice there are still uncertainties as to how to deconflict the tasks performed by the PACOM directorates from those performed by CFE-DMHA. This creates tensions between these entities.[116]

Guidance for CFE-DMHA is therefore not lacking, with the center identifying no fewer than 18 USG strategy documents of direct or indirect relevance to CFE-DMHA, including eight that provide the center with "authoritative direction."[117] However, these documents fail to provide the specific guidance that would help the center prioritize its activities. Individuals interviewed for this study mentioned that supervision—in other words, follow-up to the guidance—might even be more needed than guidance from the center's stakeholders, in particular

[111] Conversation with current or former DoD official, 2015; conversation with current or former PACOM official, 2015; phone conversation with current or former EUCOM staff, 2015; and phone conversation with current or former EUCOM staff, 2015.

[112] PACOM and CFE-DMHA, "Memorandum of Understanding Between Commander, United States Pacific Command and Director, Center for Excellence in Disaster Management and Humanitarian Assistance," July 2, 2014.

[113] PACOM, 2013.

[114] PACOM Instruction 0530.1, *Command Relationships*, Halawa Heights, Hawaii, December 2014.

[115] Conversation with current or former CFE-DMHA staff, 2015.

[116] Conversation with current or former CFE-DMHA staff, 2015; conversation with current or former DoD official, 2015.

[117] "Strategy to Task Analysis," undated.

OSD.[118] One discussant mentioned that what is missing most is proper guidance about internal CFE-DMHA governance. This would include clear—and publicly available—guidance from OSD about the roles and responsibilities of the CFE-DMHA director.[119] More generally, CFE-DMHA was described as needing more leadership and involvement from OSD. But CFE-DMHA is more likely to fall below both OSD's and PACOM's radars because of its small size.[120] One discussant suggested that an intervening agency—like the role that DSCA plays for APCSS—may be useful to help carry CFE-DMHA messages to OSD and translate strategic guidance into operationally useful instructions for the center.[121]

This lack of implementing guidance has made it possible for CFE-DMHA directors to set their own direction for the center and its relationships with OSD and PACOM (see Chapter Two).[122] On the positive side, the center's ability to adapt to each director's vision shows that it is a nimble organization, capable of switching quickly from a health to a peacekeeping focus, for example. This represents an advantage in terms of the number of funding sources that the center can attract. This is also a useful ability to have in fast-changing environments that require swift organizational adaptation. On the negative side, it has also resulted in an inability for the center to establish some form of continuity over the years. As one discussant said, "CFE has continually reinvented itself."[123] Another noted that CFE-DMHA began to have "internal implosion," with the various leaderships asking themselves what CFE-DMHA's purpose is, and this affected its ability to excel in any of its areas of work.[124]

This has adversely affected the center's reputation. In fact, establishing *any* reputation is hard when the main focus of the mission constantly changes and when CFE-DMHA cannot project a coherent image of what it does.[125] In some cases, CFE-DMHA does not project an image at all; several discussants mentioned that its name is not known in a number of humanitarian-assistance circles, including some USG ones.[126] Even with the understanding that CFE-DMHA's outreach is necessarily limited by its size, and that it cannot do activities everywhere with everyone, it does not appear to project the image that a center for excellence should.

Instability has also been difficult for CFE-DMHA's partners, who note that the uncertainty created by changing leadership makes it difficult to cooperate with the center and to

---

[118] Phone conversation with current or former CFE-DMHA staff, 2015.

[119] Conversation with current or former HADR organization staff, 2015.

[120] Conversation with current or former CFE-DMHA staff, 2015; conversation with current or former CFE-DMHA staff, 2015; and conversation with current or former CFE-DMHA staff, 2015.

[121] Conversation with current or former CFE-DMHA staff, 2015.

[122] Conversation with current or former DoD official, 2014.

[123] Phone conversation with current or former CFE-DMHA staff, 2015.

[124] Phone conversation with current or former HADR organization staff, 2015.

[125] Phone conversation with current or former CFE-DMHA staff, 2015. One discussant well acquainted with CFE-DMHA put it this way: "I am not sure what it [CFE-DMHA] is" (conversation with current or former HADR organization staff, 2015).

[126] Conversation with current or former CFE-DMHA staff, 2015; phone conversation with current or former CFE-DMHA staff, 2015. Pacific Air Forces was mentioned as an example.

know what to expect from it.[127] One discussant noted that CFE-DMHA "does not have a reputation for delivering on its mandate."[128]

Overall, when asked about CFE-DMHA's reputation, individuals interviewed for this study offered very mixed answers. This lack of consensus on CFE-DMHA's reputation suggests that some improvement is needed in that area. Comments from discussants also highlight the diversity of "reputations" that can be assessed. One discussant mentioned CFE-DMHA having a great reputation among certain DMHA actors (specifically, local DMHA personnel who work with the center) but not others.[129] Another noted that CFE-DMHA's reputation is better in the countries where it has conducted activities (e.g., Thailand, Singapore, and Indonesia) than in the countries that have a more "remote" knowledge of the organization.[130] Finally, a third discussant suggested that the success of an organization lies in part in its (and its leaders') ability to exert influence, and that CFE-DMHA cannot seem to gain traction.[131]

These mixed reviews suggest that CFE-DMHA's reputation needs to be, if not rebuilt, at least strengthened. This might require some rebranding. One discussant compared the name recognition of the "brands" APCSS and CFE-DMHA, noting that the former is attractive and the latter is not.[132] A new name—following the example of the Australian Civil-Military Centre, which changed its name from its original Asia-Pacific Civil-Military Centre of Excellence—might help give the center a new start and a chance to enhance its reputation in the humanitarian-assistance community.[133] Mixed reviews also suggest that it would be more valuable for the center to limit itself to a small set of well-defined activities and missions that it can do well, rather than be too flexible and switch its focus according to directors' preferences and available sources of funding. As described in Chapter Two, the current director is sharpening the center's focus and pursuing some rebranding.

To summarize this section on guidance, CFE-DMHA would greatly benefit from

- policy guidance that
  - gives a strategic vision for the center—not simply outlining its broad mission but stating where it should be in three to five years while remaining sufficiently flexible to allow for response to emerging opportunities
  - prioritizes the mission areas and activities the center should focus on (based on a clear understanding of the center's resource constraint)

---

[127]Conversation with current or former HADR organization staff, 2015; phone conversation with current or former HADR organization staff, 2015. As we will discuss, CFE-DMHA's commitment issues (i.e., its ability to deliver on some of its promises) is not exclusively because of its changes of direction under each new leader. These issues may also be a manning problem (when a contractor makes promises that only a government official could have made) or a funding one (when an expected source of funding for one activity does not show up).

[128]Phone conversation with current or former CFE-DMHA staff, 2015.

[129]Conversation with current or former HADR organization staff, 2015.

[130]Phone conversation with current or former DoD official, 2015; phone conversation with current or former HADR organization staff, 2015.

[131]Phone conversation with current or former HADR organization staff, 2015.

[132]Conversation with current or former CFE-DMHA staff, 2015.

[133]Conversation with current or former DoD official, 2015; phone conversation with current or former HADR organization staff, 2015.

- is synchronized between OSD and PACOM (or other CCMDs), so as to deconflict responsibility for tasks performed by CCMD staffs from those performed by CFE-DMHA
- implementing guidance that outlines
  - priority countries and organizations for CFE-DMHA to work on
  - priority activities
  - roles and responsibilities of the CFE-DMHA director, as well as the director's relationship with other stakeholders.

This new guidance would ensure that the center (1) is meeting the most-pressing needs of the oversight authority and (2) clarifies its coordinating functions and tasks vis-à-vis other USG entities engaged in DMHA. The guidance would also provide the basis for an effort at rebranding, which could involve a name change and focus on potential ways to enhance the center's reputation.

Funding

Funding fluctuations over time have caused difficulties for CFE-DMHA in achieving its missions. The CFE-DMHA's core funding averaged $5 million per year from 1998 until 2007, largely as a result of consistent allocations by congressional earmarks. Since 2008, the center has been funded through a program line item in the Navy O&M budget, which passes funding to CFE-DMHA through PACOM.[134] One discussant noted that the move from being a designated congressional earmark to a general item within the Navy O&M budget line made CFE-DMHA become more "money driven," and created competition for funds with PACOM staff.[135] Such competition worsened with the sequester, which a discussant said caused new friction between CFE-DMHA and PACOM staff.[136] CFE-DMHA's FY 2008 to FY 2015 core funding reached a high of $7.1 million in FY 2013 but has been decreasing since, down to $4 million in FY 2015 (see Figure 3.1). FY 2016 started under better auspices, with $700,000 more in core funding than the previous year.[137] To this core funding, CFE-DMHA has sought to add supplementary funding from such sources as Title 10 personnel and expenses; APRI; HIV/AIDS funding; Overseas Humanitarian, Disaster, and Civic Aid (OHDACA); USAID pandemic influenza; and others—but with mixed success (see Figure 3.1). Such supplemental funds have been inconsistent from year to year and experienced a sharp decrease from FY 2008 to FY 2014. In FY 2010, for example, the center had a $9.93 million budget, of which $5.71 million was from O&M (core) funds, $1.59 million from APRI fund, $0.39 million from PACOM's Title 10 fund, $1.32 million from USAID pandemic influenza fund, and $0.92 million from other funds. By FY 2014, the overall budget had decreased to $5.3 million, nearly all of it core funding. FY 2015 showed an uptake of supplemental funding that helped maintain CFE-DMHA's overall funding at the same level as in FY 2014 despite a decrease in

[134] Conversation with current or former PACOM officials, 2015.

[135] Conversation with current or former CFE-DMHA staff, 2015.

[136] Conversation with current or former PACOM officials, 2015.

[137] Email correspondence with CFE-DMHA staff, September 2015.

Figure 3.1
CFE-DMHA's Budget, FY 2008 to FY 2015

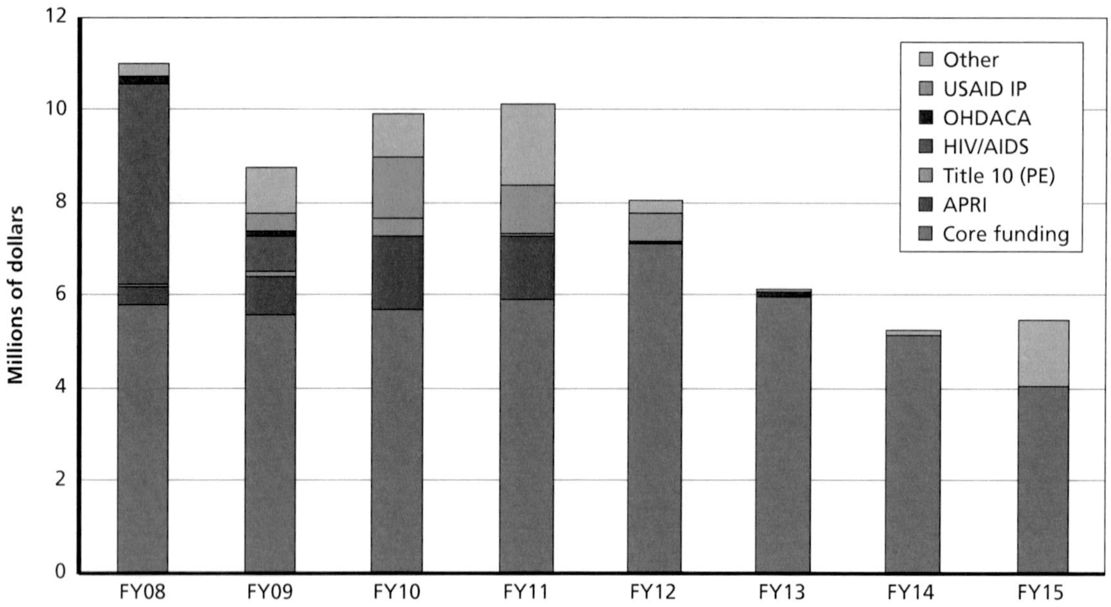

SOURCES: CFE-DMHA, CFE Funding—Historic Graph, internal briefing, Ford Island, Hawaii, undated-b; email correspondence with CFE-DMHA staff, September 2015.
NOTE: IP = influenza pandemic; PE = personnel and expenses.
RAND RR1332-3.1

core funding. In FY 2016, the center will have to find approximately $750,000 in supplemental funding to operate at the same level as in FY 2015.[138]

Although not exclusive to CFE—PDC, for instance, funds 50 percent of its budget from supplemental sources,[139] and parts of the Center for Civil-Military Relations (CCMR) work on a fully reimbursable basis[140]—heavy reliance on supplemental funding presents three important challenges that help explain the center's inability to build a reputation on a few well-mastered domains of expertise.[141] First, changing funding sources created a need to "follow the money" in determining CFE-DMHA programs. This, in turn, led to lack of continuity in programming and difficulty in planning. Second, the lack of consistency in funding sources, described by a discussant as "different pots of money with different strings attached," created its own problems.[142] OHDACA funds, for instance, must have a civilian benefit—thereby lim-

---

[138]Email correspondence with current or former CFE-DMHA staff, September 2015.

[139]Conversation with current or former HADR organization staff, 2015.

[140]Phone conversation with current or former HADR organization staff, 2015.

[141]Such challenges are not exclusive to CFE-DMHA. Some regional centers' pursuit of outside sources of funding also proves to be a significant distraction from the centers' core missions by creating a "follow-the-money" incentive and making the centers fee-for-service organizations rather than strategic tools for advancing strategic USG objectives (Larry Hanauer, Stuart E. Johnson, Christopher J. Springer, Chaoling Feng, Michael J. McNerney, Stephanie Pezard, and Shira Efron, *Evaluating the Impact of the Department of Defense Regional Centers for Security Studies*, Santa Monica, Calif.: RAND Corporation, RR-388-OSD, 2014, pp. 73–74).

[142]Phone conversation with current or former CFE-DMHA staff, 2014.

iting program flexibility, including, for example, in building civ-mil partnerships.[143] The rules for how the various funds can be used also change over the years, adding to the complexity in long-term planning or programming.[144] This makes it difficult to combine them to fund a single event and means that such an event may have to be canceled or curtailed if part of the funding falls through.[145] Finally, these additional sources of funding are rarely multiyear, making it difficult to plan or develop multiyear programs.[146] In the past, CFE-DMHA had to abandon several programs midway, after the funding did not come through.[147] Such cases not only represent missed opportunities but also undermine the credibility of CFE-DMHA with foreign partners. Inconsistent funding also makes it difficult for CFE-DMHA to deliver on its promises to its institutional partners. One discussant cited a case when CFE-DMHA offered to sponsor a meeting, only to back down because of funding issues.[148]

CFE-DMHA has one additional source of funding—at least potentially—that sets it apart from other DoD organizations. Its founding legislation (Title 10, Section 182) states

> The Secretary of Defense may accept, on behalf of the Center, donations to be used to defray the costs of the Center or to enhance the operation of the Center. Such donations may be accepted from any agency of the Federal Government, any State or local government, any foreign government, any foundation or other charitable organization (including any that is organized or operates under the laws of a foreign country), or any other private source in the United States or a foreign country.[149]

In 2004, the Deputy Secretary of Defense delegated the authority to accept donations for the center to the center's director.[150] Yet, as of 2015, the center had never used that opportunity despite some attempts made in 2005–2007 by Pete Bradford on the request of then-PACOM Commander ADM William Fallon, and again under John Goodman, to approach a number of corporations (including Google) in the hope that they may sponsor some of CFE-DMHA's activities.[151]

To summarize this section on funding:

---

[143] More specifically, "OHDACA-funded projects should not directly benefit foreign militaries or paramilitary groups. However, on a case-by-case basis, foreign militaries may be involved so long as the ultimate beneficiary is the civilian populace and the military unit has a HA [humanitarian assistance] or disaster first-responder mission" (DSCA, "Humanitarian Assistance and Mine Action Programs," in *Security Assistance Management Manual*, last revised October 1, 2015).

[144] Phone conversation with current or former CFE-DMHA staff, 2014.

[145] Phone conversation with current or former CFE-DMHA staff, 2014.

[146] Phone conversation with current or former CFE-DMHA staff, 2014. ODHACA funds can be executed over two years, but they can also be redirected to other emergencies (for instance, the Ebola outbreak), and, as a result, may become unavailable after one year. This issue, however, is not specific to CFE-DMHA and is a perennial problem that equally affects other DoD entities involved in security cooperation and HADR.

[147] Phone conversation with current or former CFE-DMHA staff, 2014.

[148] Phone conversation with current or former HADR organization staff, 2015.

[149] U.S.C., Title 10, Section 182 (d).

[150] U.S. Deputy Secretary of Defense, "Memorandum for Director, Center of Excellence in Disaster Management and Humanitarian Assistance; Subject: Authority to Accept Donations," May 10, 2004.

[151] Conversation with current or former CFE-DMHA staff, 2015; phone conversation with current or former CFE-DMHA staff, 2015; and conversation with current or former PACOM officials, 2015.

- CFE-DMHA needs consistent long-term core funding to mitigate the uncertainties and lack of focus created by varying levels of supplemental funding. Although we realize this is a challenge for every DoD organization in the current budget environment, the instability it creates is particularly damaging to organizations like CFE-DMHA whose primary objectives include building partnership capacity and long-term relationships with myriad international partners.
- CFE-DMHA should select sources of additional funding that closely fit its core missions. This could help it avoid some sudden shifts in focus that have characterized it in the past. At the risk of turning down needed funds for potentially valuable programs, CFE-DMHA may wish to refrain from seeking project-specific fee-for-service funds specifically to prevent such funds from diverting the center from its core missions.
- Strategy and resources need to match. CFE-DMHA cannot address an unchanging mandate covering a broad array of DMHA-related areas with decreasing funding.
- CFE-DMHA should take advantage of its ability to accept donations to explore alternative sources of funding—but only if this would enable activities that are consistent with its core missions.

Manning

Three intertwining manning problems have inhibited CFE-DMHA's ability to accomplish its broad mandate from its inception: (1) with respect to "troops to tasks," the center has never been sufficiently manned to accomplish its broad mandate; (2) an unhealthy government-to-contractor employee ratio inhibits the center's ability to address inherently governmental functions; and (3) a lack of DMHA subject-matter expertise, among the entire staff, that would be expected from a center for excellence.

CFE-DMHA has had, on average, 33 personnel since opening. A 2009 manpower review suggested that more than twice as many personnel would be necessary to fulfill the center's entire mandate (see Chapter Four).[152] Numerous discussants emphasized that the center's small size created challenges in relation to its broad mandate.[153] One discussant described trying to get CFE-DMHA to do all that it should with its current means as "spreading peanut butter," resulting in CFE-DMHA overpromising and eventually disappointing.[154] A number of chronic issues snowball from the small size of the center. For example, knowing that it would not be able to deliver on increased demands, the center does not necessarily try to attract new work, which in turn inhibits its ability to build its reputation.[155] One discussant even suggested that CFE-DMHA is too small to be viable as a stand-alone enterprise.[156]

CFE-DMHA staff numbers, particularly among government employees, have been diminishing in recent years (see Figure 3.2). One PACOM discussant described CFE-DMHA's

---

[152] COE-DMHA, 2012b, slide 17.

[153] Conversation with current or former CFE-DMHA staff, 2015; phone conversation with current or former CFE-DMHA staff, 2014; phone conversation with current or former CFE-DMHA staff, 2015; conversation with current or former CFE-DMHA staff, 2015; and phone conversation with current or former CFE-DMHA staff, 2014.

[154] Phone conversation with current or former CFE-DMHA staff, 2015; conversation with current or former CFE-DMHA staff, 2015.

[155] Conversation with current or former CFE-DMHA staff, 2015.

[156] Phone conversation with current or former CFE-DMHA staff, 2014.

Figure 3.2
CFE-DMHA Staff Numbers and Types, 1994–2014

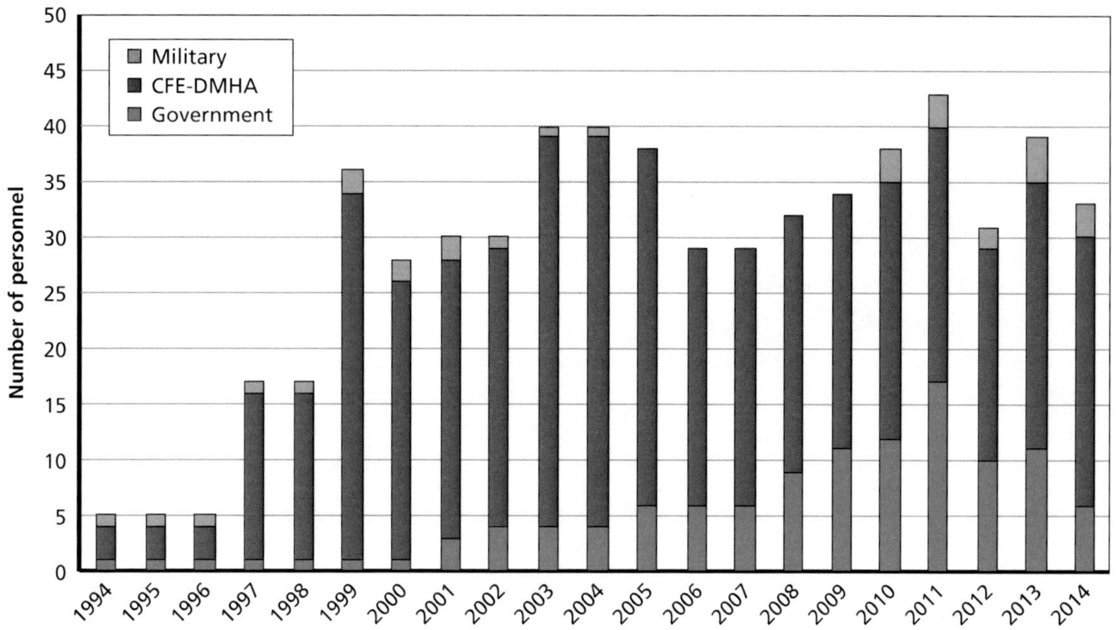

SOURCES: CFE-DMHA, undated-e, slide 1; and CFE-DMHA, 2015g.
RAND RR1332-3.2

decreasing staffing as a "slow bleed."[157] As of mid-2015, CFE-DMHA's staff consisted of six DoD civilian billets, including two civilian overhires (one of whom will depart in 2016); one Senior Executive Service (SES) position, for the director;[158] one reservist (whose position went away in October 2015); and one part-time military, who was seconded from Pacific Air Forces two days a week.[159] Support contractors filled the remaining 21.5 staff positions. At the time of writing, the center was pursuing a plan to add three USG civilians and offset this by reducing contractors by the same number.[160]

In addition to size, the government-to-contractor balance has been an important issue for CFE-DMHA. Contractors have always largely outnumbered civilians by nearly four to one at the center. Although contractors can benefit government organizations through hiring flexibility and agility, as well as subject-matter expertise,[161] an overreliance on contractors can impede the ability of a government organization to address inherently governmental functions. One result of this is that CFE-DMHA must cover such functions with a small governmental

---

[157] Conversation with current or former PACOM official, 2015.

[158] One of the seven positions is for a director. This position was still vacant at the time of writing, as the interim director was still formally employed by PACOM J9.

[159] Phone conversation with current or former CFE-DMHA staff, 2015.

[160] CFE-DMHA, untitled briefing slides, internal document, Ford Island, Hawaii, July 14, 2015d.

[161] Conversation with current or former CFE-DMHA staff, 2015; and conversation with current or former CFE-DMHA staff, 2015. One of these discussants noted that a mix of contractors and government people is an asset because experience only lasts a certain amount of time, and contractors give the center the ability to reach and touch SMEs when it needs it (conversation with current or former CFE-DMHA staff, 2015).

staff that is both stretched and not necessarily best employed in these functions.[162] Even more important for CFE-DMHA's mission, contractors cannot represent the USG during engagement activities.[163] Numerous discussants noted that the lack of government representation for CFE-DMHA can be problematic.[164] One discussant cited a case in which a CFE-DMHA contractor committed the center to run an activity with a partner country despite lacking the authority to make such a commitment.[165] CFE-DMHA government staff also must travel extensively. A representative of another DMHA organization noted that one reason CFE-DMHA was not more involved in that organization's activities is that all of CFE-DMHA's "shooters" are always deployed somewhere, and it is difficult to get them to come to events.[166]

Among the specific challenges that a large ratio of contractors to government employees can create are time the government employees must spend on management;[167] the difficulties CFE-DMHA has in redirecting staff, as needed, in the face of contract limitations;[168] high levels of turnover, reducing the overall stability of the organization;[169] lack of a "government face," which can be detrimental to CFE-DMHA in its requests for funding;[170] and a higher labor cost for the organization, because contractors are more expensive than government employees.[171] In sum, contractors can provide particular areas of expertise as needs arise but have failed to provide reliability or consistency and are not as cost-effective as government employees.

---

[162] Phone conversation with current or former CFE-DMHA staff, 2014; phone conversation with current or former EUCOM staff, 2015.

[163] One mentioned meetings that only government personnel can attend, such as meetings on U.S. prioritization (phone conversation with current or former CFE-DMHA staff, 2014). Another said that contractors cannot be in coordinating or planning roles, because coordinating between different government entities requires a government employee, especially given the risk of sharing information with contractors about activities that may later be contracted. (Phone conversation with current or former HADR organization staff, 2015.)

[164] Phone conversation with current or former CFE-DMHA staff, 2014; phone conversation with current or former HADR organization staff, 2015.

[165] Phone conversation with current or former HADR organization staff, 2015.

[166] Conversation with current or former HADR organization staff, 2015.

[167] Conversation with current or former CFE-DMHA staff, 2015. As one discussant put it, "You have to be very specific on your requirement with contractors, otherwise you get the wrong people" (conversation with current or former CFE-DMHA staff, 2015).

[168] Conversation with current or former CFE-DMHA staff, 2015. A representative of another HADR organization noted that having a CFE-DMHA contractor participate in the organization's events was difficult, given resulting questions, such as whether participation was covered in the contract and whom should be billed for it (conversation with current or former HADR organization staff, 2015).

[169] Conversation with current or former CFE-DMHA staff, 2015.

[170] As one discussant put it, "You have to show that you have government people" (phone conversation with current or former CFE-DMHA staff, 2014). Another discussant made a similar point highlighting the "hierarchy in DoD between military personnel, civilian personnel, contractors (in that order)" and the "lack of respect for contractors" hurting CFE-DMHA as an organization within the OSD chain of authority (phone conversation with current or former EUCOM staff, 2015).

[171] Conversation with current or former CFE-DMHA staff, 2015. This was also one of the conclusions of the 2012 PACOM business case analysis (Andrew Wilcox and Rick Chambers, "Center of Excellence in Disaster Management and Humanitarian Assistance (COE-DMHA): Business Case Analysis," briefing slides, Ford Island, Hawaii: Center for Excellence in Disaster Management and Humanitarian Assistance, undated, slide 6).

The research team also heard contrasting views regarding the quality of the contracting function at CFE-DMHA. According to one discussant, CFE-DMHA's ability to choose candidates is limited, as the contractor offers one or two candidates for a position and suggests making changes if the individual "doesn't work out."[172] Another discussant, however, found the current contracting system to be adequate and argued against CFE-DMHA micromanaging the contractor hiring process.[173] Whatever the case may be, and as long as CFE-DMHA keeps a high ratio of contractors to government employees, the center would benefit from having a skilled contracting officer on staff to give its leadership more control over the contract and the types of individuals hired.

Past assessments of CFE-DMHA have repeatedly underscored manning issues. A 2009 PACOM manpower review recommended converting some contractor positions into governmental ones to ensure that the center would have enough personnel to perform inherently governmental functions and to reduce personnel costs.[174] The review concluded that CFE-DMHA would need 69 staff members to execute its mission, including 45 DoD civilians (up from 11) and 24 contractors (up from 23).[175] A 2010 PACOM IG review "identified additional manpower requirements to ensure compliance with DoD program directives."[176] In 2012, the PACOM-directed BCA identified both the small size of the CFE-DMHA staff and the contractor-to-government ratio as problems.[177] The BCA recommended that CFE-DMHA have 15 civilian positions and seven military.[178]

Change finally occurred when, in September 2012, PACOM supported 31 USG billets for CFE-DMHA, as well as unfunded international and interagency representatives.[179] These changes, however, were never implemented, because of the prospect of sequestration and CFE-DMHA's "operational pause."[180]

As noted earlier, CFE-DMHA has only six billets for government civilians and has been overcoming the shortage of government staff with two overhires and three military personnel (including one part time). Two members of this "extra staff" (one overhire and one military) were slated to sunset in 2015 and 2016.[181] According to one discussant, five to six additional

---

[172] Conversation with current or former DoD official, 2015.

[173] Conversation with current or former CFE-DMHA staff, 2015.

[174] COE-DMHA, 2012b, slide 17.

[175] CFE-DMHA, undated-c, slide 1.

[176] The research team did not have access to PACOM IG reports.

[177] Wilcox and Chambers, undated, slide 6.

[178] CFE-DMHA, undated-c, slides 1, 4, and 5. At the time, CFE-DMHA was operating with ten DoD civilians, two military, and 19 contractors.

[179] CFE-DMHA, undated-c, slide 6.

[180] Conversation with current or former CFE-DMHA staff, 2015. "Operational pause" is the name that was given to CFE-DMHA's transition phase following the resignation of CFE-DMHA Director John Goodman. CFE-DMHA's operations were curtailed while the center restructured and developed a new strategy. Since CFE-DMHA had committed to a number of events that had already been approved, however, there was little of an actual "pause" as the center's remaining staff worked to deliver on these commitments (email correspondence with current or former CFE-DMHA staff, September 2015).

[181] Phone conversation with current or former CFE-DMHA staff, 2015. Technically, three will go away (one overhire and the two military positions), but one of the military positions is the current interim director, who will be replaced by a director, and since the government billet for the director exists, CFE-DMHA will not really be losing a staff member.

civilian positions (ensuring a ratio closer to one civilian for two contractors) would be needed to ensure that CFE-DMHA's DoD staff can cover all inherently governmental functions that the center needs to fulfill.[182] More broadly, CFE-DMHA's current staff levels do not allow it to fulfill all the missions it "shall" conduct according to the Title 10 legislation that authorized it (see Appendix A).

CFE-DMHA has also had some difficulty in obtaining the necessary expertise for its missions[183] because of three main problems: the center is too small to have a dedicated expert on each domain; the staff's background lacks diversity; and, according to a number of discussants, CFE-DMHA has not attracted the level of subject-matter expertise that would qualify it to be a true center for excellence.

First, because it has only six DoD employee billets, CFE-DMHA cannot allow its civilian staff to become too specialized, since it also must be versatile. As a result, most staff members are generalists.[184] One discussant had issues with "decision-makers [government employees] at CFE-DMHA [who] are not the SMEs."[185] This can damage CFE-DMHA credibility, because some staff members may end up taking charge of activities for which they are not recognized specialists—either because an appropriate contractor could not be found or because the activity took place during a gap between contracts.[186] Paradoxically, the few civilian employees with specialized skills sometimes cannot be used for the activities that would require these skills because they are too busy doing inherently governmental functions at the center, such as planning or budgeting.[187]

Second, several interviewees mentioned the center's staff lacks diversity in its experience, an ongoing effect of the shift imparted by Goodman toward a staff with a military rather than civilian humanitarian background.[188] The loss of staff with experience at the CDC, the United Nations, NGOs, or in academia was said to have hampered CFE-DMHA's ability to have a "holistic" view of civ-mil relations and to adequately cover a number of issues important for disaster management.[189] For instance, in the mid-2000s, no one on staff had worked on the 2004 Indian Ocean tsunami, which was the biggest disaster at that point in time.[190] The imbalance between military and civilian practitioners is particularly problematic for main-

---

[182] Phone conversation with current or former CFE-DMHA staff, 2015.

[183] This was an issue that was already underlined in the 2012 BCA, which concluded that there was a "lack of sufficient SMEs" (Wilcox and Chambers, undated, slide 6).

[184] Phone conversation with current or former CFE-DMHA staff, 2014.

[185] Phone conversation with current or former CFE-DMHA staff, 2015.

[186] Phone conversation with current or former CFE-DMHA staff, 2014.

[187] Phone conversation with current or former CFE-DMHA staff, 2014. It is important to note that there is some disagreement about what constitutes an inherently governmental task and what contractors can, and cannot, do. The legal and administrative issues that CFE-DMHA experienced in the past, however, suggest that the center may want to adopt a conservative approach (i.e., have government employees do tasks where there is uncertainty) in this regard.

[188] Phone conversation with current or former CFE-DMHA staff, 2014.

[189] Phone conversation with current or former CFE-DMHA staff, 2015; conversation with current or former CFE-DMHA staff, 2015; and phone conversation with current or former AFRICOM official, 2015. This is not a hard rule, however, as demonstrated by the recent hiring of a well-regarded academician.

[190] Phone conversation with current or former EUCOM staff, 2015.

taining DMHA expertise, where processes change quickly and knowledge becomes obsolete quickly.[191]

Having staff with a predominantly military background also deprives CFE-DMHA of an opportunity envisioned in its initial plan in 1994, to develop reachback into civilian organizations, such as USAID, the CDC, and the United Nations.[192] It hampers the center's ability to engage civilian partners, as many NGOs, and even some international organizations and foreign civilian agencies, prefer to avoid the image of working closely with the U.S. military. Moreover, center staff with long tenures at civilian organizations or recent humanitarian experience can provide reliable interlocutors between military organizations and foreign partners with whom the staff have long-standing relationships. Overall, working with USAID and a wide variety of international organizations and NGOs to improve civ-mil coordination is most easily and effectively pursued through an organization perceived as having strong civilian ties and that can forge, and consistently sustain, personal and organizational relationships over an extended period.

Third, another recurrent question, raised in the 2012 BCA as well, is whether CFE-DMHA's SMEs are indeed "person[s] with bona fide expert knowledge about what it takes to do a particular job."[193] Although there were several very positive reviews of CFE-DMHA staff competence—one interviewee claimed that all contractors had great experience with a broad set of disciplines,[194] while another said all civilian employees are extremely knowledgeable at what they do[195]—there were also concerns that the center has too few PhDs and too few academic publications to be a center for excellence.[196] More generally, CFE-DMHA was said to have problems hiring and retaining top-quality SMEs, which, according to some, was partially because of difficulty in attracting to Hawaii candidates with sufficient on-the-ground experience.[197] One solution mentioned was to use excepted service authorities to hire well-respected SMEs, as this system allows some organizations to negotiate contracts with experts in the field and bring them in with no overhead.[198] Whether the CFE-DMHA director should also be a SME has been debated and is best understood in relation to the other characteristics deemed necessary (see Box 3.2). Lastly, it is unclear whether knowledge is institutionalized at

---

[191] Phone conversation with current or former CFE-DMHA staff, 2015.

[192] Phone conversation with current or former CFE-DMHA staff, 2014. CFE-DMHA was, for instance, able to facilitate a relationship with the CDC.

[193] U.S. Office of Personnel Management, 2007, glossary. We realize the limits of this definition, however, since that publication's glossary defines neither what it means by *bona fide* or *expert knowledge*.

[194] Conversation with current or former CFE-DMHA staff, 2015.

[195] Conversation with current or former PACOM official, 2015.

[196] As of 2015, the center had only one PhD on staff. Phone conversation with current or former CFE-DMHA staff, 2015; conversation with current or former CFE-DMHA staff, 2015. See also the discussion of the center's reputation. A U.S. Army Training and Doctrine Command document defines an Army center of excellence as "a premier organization that creates the highest standards of achievement in an assigned sphere of expertise by generating synergy through an effective and efficient combination and integration of functions, while reinforcing the unique requirements and capabilities" (U.S. Army Training and Doctrine Command Regulation 10-5-5, *United States Army Combined Arms Support Command and Sustainment Center of Excellence*, Fort Monroe, Va.: Department of the Army, Headquarters, September 10, 2010, p. 10).

[197] Conversation with current or former PACOM official, 2015; phone conversation with current or former CFE-DMHA staff, 2015; conversation with current or former CFE-DMHA staff, 2015; phone conversation with current or former EUCOM staff, 2015.

[198] Phone conversation with current or former CFE-DMHA staff, 2015.

Box 3.2. What Traits Should a CFE-DMHA Director Have?

The RAND team, recognizing the importance of the role that the CFE-DMHA director plays in the organization, particularly in the absence of specific implementation guidance, asked several discussants (including current and former CFE-DMHA staff) what they believed would be the ideal profile of a CFE-DMHA director. We note the attributes deemed most essential:

• Many discussants said that the director should be, first and foremost, a "good manager of people" and have good leadership skills.[1]

• Discussants also emphasized that the director should have a good understanding of civ-mil relationships to ensure that CFE-DMHA has credibility in both sectors.[2] This means, in particular, being very fluent in interagency lingo, including military lingo,[3] while also being able to engage civilians when necessary (e.g., when engaging partners particularly wary of U.S. military involvement).[4]

• Discussants said that the director could have a military or a civilian background. One discussant, however, suggested the director should have a background in humanitarian work that also successfully included the military, given how focused on military background the staff currently is.[5]

• Discussants were divided on whether the director should also be a SME.[6] Some argued that relevant experience in disaster and crisis management and accompanying credibility is "critical" and that CFE-DMHA needs a director who can understand the mission.[7] We conclude that it is preferred that a CFE-DMHA director have some degree of DMHA expertise.

• All said that the CFE-DMHA director needed "gravitas" to engage CCMD commanders, undersecretaries and above, ambassadors, and partner-nation leadership.[8] This would require the director to be an official with the equivalent (or past) rank of general officer, ambassador, or a member of the SES or Senior Foreign Service, if only to be at the same level as the PACOM J9 director (SES) and the APCSS director (who has the rank of lieutenant-general).[9]

• Finally, the appointment of the CFE-DMHA director would benefit from being an open and competitive search with full coordination among the key stakeholders.[10]

NOTES

[1] Conversation with current or former HADR organization staff, 2015; conversation with current or former CFE-DMHA staff, 2015; conversation with current or former PACOM official, 2015.

[2] Conversation with current or former HADR organization staff, 2015.

[3] Conversation with current or former PACOM official, 2015.

[4] Conversation with current or former PACOM official, 2015.

[5] Phone conversation with current or former CFE-DMHA staff, 2015.

[6] Phone conversation with current or former CFE-DMHA staff, 2015; conversation with current or former CFE-DMHA staff, 2015; and conversation with current or former CFE-DMHA staff, 2015.

[7] Phone conversation with current or former CFE-DMHA staff, 2015; conversation with current or former CFE-DMHA staff, 2015.

[8] Conversation with current or former CFE-DMHA staff, 2015; conversation with current or former CFE-DMHA staff, 2015.

[9] Conversation with current or former CFE-DMHA staff, 2015; conversation with current or former CFE-DMHA staff, 2015.

[10] Conversation with current or former CFE-DMHA staff, 2014.

CFE-DMHA or belongs to a handful of individuals on whom the center relies. Individuals interviewed for this study repeatedly mentioned—in extremely positive terms—one or two individuals at CFE-DMHA. This raises questions whether they represent institutional knowledge or points of failure.

To summarize this section on manning: CFE-DMHA has serious manning issues that have been undermining its performance for years. Despite several previous assessments—including the 2012 BCA—underscoring these issues, no decisive changes were made, and CFE-DMHA is still suffering from problems now made worse by further reductions in funding and staff size. To start addressing these issues, CFE-DMHA needs several things:

- The center needs widely recognized DMHA experts on staff with extensive and recent experience in civ-mil coordination in disasters. CFE-DMHA, in particular, needs more staff with recent humanitarian and disaster experience and who are established experts in their fields.
- The center needs a civilian face to the organization with staff who can maintain positive relationships with stakeholders, especially foreign partners. This is particularly important for those NGOs wary of associating themselves too closely with the U.S. military.
- The center needs an adequate mix of USG and contract employees. CFE-DMHA needs more government employees to represent official U.S. policy to foreign audiences and to maintain an efficient organization while pursuing its missions. The current director is seeking to make some strides in this area, but much more needs to be done.
- The center needs a director who (1) is a proven, effective leader and manager, (2) has executive-level status, and (3) has experience in humanitarian assistance. Hiring the director should be open and competitive, with full coordination among the key stakeholders.

Mission Support

CFE-DMHA's mission-support functions, such as comptroller, contracts, personnel, security, records management, logistics, and travel, are inadequately filled—or not filled at all—creating repeated challenges for the center.[199] CFE-DMHA does not have the government billets that would allow it to fill those administrative functions of an inherently governmental nature. This raises the question of whether it can even function as an independent center and what it takes (in terms of the functions that need to be fulfilled) to run one. Box 3.3 examines some general rules from the relevant literature on the characteristics of effective organizations.

In recent years, CFE-DMHA has lost some of its mission-support functions to PACOM—which is good news considering the small size of the center's staff, but bad news for the center's agility and control over its operations. CFE-DMHA, for instance, went from using a commercial website and mail system to relying on PACOM for information technology—a change that saved personnel and financial resources but also resulted in a loss of flexibility for CFE-DMHA.[200] This has also been problematic for CFE-DMHA's role as a repository of DMHA knowledge and information, since the size of its shared drive was drastically reduced—forc-

---

[199] Phone conversation with current or former CFE-DMHA staff, 2015.

[200] Conversation with current or former CFE-DMHA staff, 2015.

Box 3.3. Characteristics of Effective Organizations

Although there is no single set of principles that define an effective organization, research has identified general principles that are often associated with more-effective organizations. In a critical review of the research on the effectiveness of government organizations, Rainey and Steinbauer emphasize several components or conditions that can promote organizational effectiveness.[1] For CFE-DMHA, these conditions would include (1) oversight organizations that support the organizational mission and demonstrate a vested interest in mission accomplishment; (2) effective relationships with multiple stakeholders, including partner nations, civilian and military humanitarian organizations, and contractors (e.g., SMEs); (3) a clearly stated mission that is attractive to DoD and CFE-DMHA's organizational members that emphasizes CFE-DMHA's value to DoD and other key stakeholders; (4) a stable leadership across multiple levels of CFE-DMHA, composed of people who are committed to the mission, have the capability to establish clear organizational goals and objectives, and can effectively adapt to political and administrative constraints; and (5) qualified and professional staff who have the necessary expertise and commitment to support CFE-DMHA's goals and mission.

Brewer and Seldon examined many of the factors proposed by Rainey and Steinbauer, measuring organizational effectiveness by surveying employees from 23 of the largest federal agencies.[2] Brewer and Seldon measured organizational effectiveness by assessing employees' perceptions of the quality and productivity of their work units, as well as perceptions of how fairly employees were treated. Among the variables that predicted organizational effectiveness were an organizational culture that promotes teamwork, high standards, and fairness; a human-capital program that selects and retains a sufficient number of highly qualified and capable staff with the right knowledge, skills, and abilities; and effective leadership that provides structure for work groups to complete tasks. Brewer and Seldon also found that organizations with too many management levels, termed *red tape*, were less effective.

ing it to constantly choose what electronic information and documents to keep or not. CFE-DMHA now works closely with PACOM's knowledge-management team.[201]

More critically, repeated allegations of improper use of funds by CFE-DMHA have resulted in the center eventually losing, in 2012, the ability to manage its own funds. Its comptroller function is now located at PACOM, which assigned a point of contact for CFE-DMHA to follow up on its financial matters.[202] One individual interviewed for this study noted that, as a result of this shift, CFE-DMHA lost its ability to respond quickly to requests for venue or

---

[201] Conversation with current or former CFE-DMHA staff, 2015.

[202] Conversation with current or former PACOM officials, 2015.

Box 3.3.—Continued

The findings in both Rainey and Steinbauer and Brewer and Seldon are broadly consistent with research on high-performance work practices (HPWPs). HPWPs include training, selectivity, promotions, rewards for employees, teamwork, information sharing, job security, organizational assessment, and organizational culture. When used effectively, such practices can enhance employee and organizational performance. For example, a meta-analysis of 92 studies that included results from analyses of 19,000 organizations showed that HPWPs generally have a modest but positive impact on organizational performance.[3] These practices were found to have a stronger effect on organizational performance when combined as a system. This finding suggests that efforts should focus on combining multiple strategies, such as human-capital management strategies[4] and organizational assessment,[5] to enhance performance.

NOTES

[1] Hal G. Rainey and Paula Steinbauer, "Galloping Elephants: Developing Elements of a Theory of Effective Government Organizations," *Journal of Public Administration Research and Theory*, Vol. 9, No. 1, 1999.

[2] G. A. Brewer and S. C. Selden, "Why Elephants Gallop: Assessing and Predicting Organizational Performance in Federal Agencies," *Journal of Public Administration Research and Theory*, Vol. 10, No. 4, 2000.

[3] J. Combs, Y. Liu, A. Hall, and D. Ketchen, "How Much Do High-Performance Work Practices Matter? A Meta-Analysis of Their Effects on Organizational Performance," *Personnel Psychology*, Vol. 59, No. 3, 2006.

[4] See, for instance, K. Jiang, D. P. Lepak, J. Hu, and J. C. Baer, "How Does Human Resource Management Influence Organizational Outcomes? A Meta-Analytic Investigation of Mediating Mechanisms," *Academy of Management Journal*, Vol. 55, No. 6, 2012.

[5] See, for instance, T. W. Muldrow, T. Buckley, and B. W. Schay, "Creating High-Performance Organizations in the Public Sector," *Human Resource Management*, Vol. 41, No. 3, 2002.

travel packages and to turn out funding documents quickly.[203] There are mixed opinions as to whether this arrangement makes PACOM sufficiently responsive to the center's needs.[204]

One element beyond dispute, however, is that CFE-DMHA, which is a very small organization, must compete with other PACOM staff organizations for priority and resources, and it seems inevitable that some small tasks that are essential to CFE-DMHA are not addressed in a timely manner by PACOM. At the same time, if CFE-DMHA maintains its current size, it is unrealistic to expect that it can take over these administrative functions.

To summarize this section on mission support, such functions are critical for CFE-DMHA to effectively operate as a center. The lack or inadequacy of such support functions has contributed to the demise of successive CFE-DMHA directors. We offer recommendations for improving the CFE-DMHA support functions center:

- Resource CFE-DMHA to ensure that it can properly fund the functions that have shown serious shortcomings in the past: comptroller, contracts, and travel. Delegating some of

---

[203]Conversation with current or former CFE-DMHA staff, 2015.

[204]Conversation with current or former CFE-DMHA staff, 2015; phone conversation with current or former CFE-DMHA staff, 2015.

these functions to PACOM hampers the flexibility of the center, and ensuring that the center has skilled staff for handling these matters would go a long way toward solving accountability and competency problems.

- For those functions that cannot be returned to CFE-DMHA, the center and PACOM should review the MOU on functions that PACOM committed to provide to CFE-DMHA to assess how effectively PACOM has done so and how it can improve.

Conclusion: CFE-DMHA Fulfills Important Requirements but Needs More Focus, Fewer Missions, and More Guidance and Resources

Our assessment of how CFE-DMHA performs its activities suggests three conclusions. First, the capability that CFE-DMHA represents is important not only for PACOM but also for DoD as a whole. In other words, if CFE-DMHA did not exist, another organization would have to fill this role of providing education, training, and research in civ-mil DMHA operations. The need for such activities in the region remains. CFE-DMHA offers unique capabilities in its courses, research products, and relationships in the Asia-Pacific region, providing value to DoD and addressing important needs. CFE-DMHA is also particularly well positioned to engage both civilians and militaries thanks to its special congressional authority, which would be lost if CFE-DMHA disappeared. Hence, despite its difficult history and uneven performance in civ-mil DMHA operations, we recommend that CFE-DMHA not be abolished.

Second, given our interviews and the few metrics available, it appears that CFE-DMHA's performance has been uneven, suggesting that the center should focus on activities where it holds a comparative advantage and drop the activities that it cannot perform well or that are performed by other organizations (an issue we discuss in the next chapter).

Third, the center's mission and resources are misaligned and have been for years (as several reports and assessments have shown). This suggests that the status quo is not tenable and that guidance, funding, manning, and mission support must change if the center is to function properly and avoid the turmoil that has plagued it since its inception. As described in Chapter Two, the current director has indeed acknowledged that the status quo is untenable and has sought to make important progress toward ameliorating the center's endemic problems by directly addressing its guidance, funding, manning, and mission support shortfalls.

These ongoing efforts may yield some improvements in the functioning and stability of the center in its current form; the extent of improvement can only be measured over time. But solving these problems will not fully answer the question of what the center should become. We turn to this question next.

CHAPTER FOUR

Missions, Geographic Focus, and Courses of Action

We have argued that CFE-DMHA and the capabilities it brings to the DMHA environment should be retained, but that the center's history of dysfunction, lack of focus, and uneven effectiveness is likely to continue if the status quo is maintained. While the current director has made important progress in improving the operation and focus of CFE-DMHA by better aligning its activities with available resources, its future success in meeting the needs of DoD and working with the humanitarian community depends on fundamental change in the center's form. This chapter describes that change by addressing the three questions presented in the introductory chapter: (1) Which mission(s) should CFE-DMHA emphasize at this time? (2) What should be CFE-DMHA's geographic focus? (3) Which courses of action best position CFE-DMHA to pursue its mission(s) and focus?

As we delve into these questions, we note a number of caveats regarding the scope of our work. First, in reviewing CFE-DMHA's Title 10 missions, we identified other DoD and USG organizations that pursue all or part of a mission assigned to the center. When identifying overlap, we assumed that the other organization accomplishes the mission adequately to the point that CFE-DMHA could deemphasize it, at least in the near term, but we did not evaluate the efforts of these other organizations. Second, we reviewed only cursorily the DMHA and civ-mil coordination needs of other regions and CCMDs to get a sense of global requirements. A more systematic, in-depth understanding of these requirements is needed. Finally, we reviewed several courses of action to enable general consideration of future options for the center. Though the courses of action incorporate broad treatment of future status and general magnitude of required resources, it was beyond the scope of the study to assess in depth the specific partner institutions with which CFE-DMHA might merge, costs of specific courses of action, or how a transition might occur to execute a course of action.

The Center Should Emphasize a Subset of Its Assigned Title 10 Missions

Our research has led us to conclude that CFE-DMHA is neither resourced nor best positioned at this time to equally emphasize all of the missions assigned to it in Title 10, Section 182. As we observed in Chapter One, the field of DMHA has benefited from the addition of several new parties, including ones associated with DoD. As demand has grown, other organizations have provided needed capacity. The principal civilian agencies that perform these missions have greatly expanded their training and oversight of the military in DMHA. This means that many missions assigned by Congress to CFE-DMHA are also performed in part or in their entirety by other organizations, at times with more resources. Moreover, as we noted in reviewing CFE-DMHA's history in Chapter Two, the center already has curtailed its activities in many of these areas. However, CFE-DMHA may have a competitive advantage and be positioned to add unique value to DMHA missions for which demand has not been satisfied.

Our recommendations for CFE-DMHA mission emphases are temporal in nature and do not preclude the center from conducting some activities related to missions it might deemphasize, or from placing greater emphasis on them in the future. Agility has been a notable attribute of the center throughout its existence. Though the tendency for directors to significantly shift CFE-DMHA's focus has diluted its effectiveness, the ability of the staff to respond to these changes has been commendable. Maintaining this agility would help CFE-DMHA respond to new and emerging requirements and allow it to address stated Title 10 missions if they become greater priorities for the center. Hence, our review of missions does not suggest that DoD seek revisions to the Title 10 authority itself. Rather, we suggest that CFE-DMHA should receive guidance from OSD that directs which missions should receive priority at any given time. The authority provides the center and the Secretary of Defense with a unique means of training and engaging with partners in DMHA and is important to retain. However, because of CFE-DMHA's existence through statute, DoD may need to consult Congress about any plans for changing CFE-DMHA orientation.

As seen in Appendix A, Title 10, Section 182(b), identifies five missions:

- (1): Provide and facilitate education, training, and research in civil-military operations, particularly operations that require international disaster management and humanitarian assistance and operations that require coordination between the Department of Defense and other agencies.
- (2): Make available high-quality disaster management and humanitarian assistance in response to disasters.
- (3): Provide and facilitate education, training, interagency coordination, and research on the following additional matters:
  - (A): Management of the consequences of nuclear, biological, and chemical events.
  - (B): Management of the consequences of terrorism.
  - (C): Appropriate roles for the reserve components.
  - (D): Meeting requirements for information in connection with regional and global disasters, including the use of advanced communications technology as a virtual library.
  - (E): Tropical medicine.
- (4): Develop a repository of disaster risk indicators for the Asia-Pacific region.
- (5): Perform such other missions as the Secretary of Defense may specify.

Missions 1, 2, 4, and 5 are stated in general terms, while mission 3 specifies the types of disasters or matters that CFE-DMHA should address. The missions were intentionally arrayed to overlap, reflecting the fact that real-world response operations can be complex and may contain a combination of missions.[1] Note that in some cases the language specifies activities—such as education, training, interagency coordination, and research—to accomplish the mis-

---

[1]   Phone conversation with current or former CFE-DMHA staff, 2014. Even natural disasters can have unforeseen consequences and cascading effects, such as the Japanese Tomodachi disaster in March 2011.

sion. Finally, as indicated in Chapter Two, CFE-DMHA adopted a peacekeeping operation-training mission in 2000, but this was dropped from the center's portfolio several years later.[2]

Chapter Three analyzed CFE-DMHA activity categories and recommended activities that CFE-DMHA should continue to emphasize and those it should deemphasize, at least until its resources and expertise enable it to adequately address them. The following discussion associates the recommended activities with the Title 10 CFE-DMHA missions the activities should support. Table 4.1 identifies missions for CFE-DMHA to address and a summary of the justification for our conclusions on these matters.

Missions CFE-DMHA Should Continue to Emphasize

"Mission (1)—Provide and facilitate education, training, and research in civil-military operations, particularly operations that require international disaster management and humanitarian assistance and operations that require coordination between the Department of Defense and other

Table 4.1
Title 10 Missions CFE-DMHA Should Emphasize

Missions Assigned to CFE in 10 USC 182	Should CFE Emphasize the Mission at This Time?	Why or Why Not?
(1) Provide/facilitate education, training, and research on international civ-mil DMHA operations	Yes	CFE maintains leverage and competitive advantage using special authority to work with partners
(2) Make available high-quality DMHA in response to disasters	Partially	Disaster response capacity in DoD has grown, but CFE can provide expertise and advice on research-based best practices to CCMD or Joint Task Force commanders
(3) Provide/facilitate education, training, interagency coordination, and research on: (3)(A) CBRN consequence management	No	DTRA and other agencies cover this
(3)(B) Terrorism consequence management	No	U.S. law enforcement and military agencies focus on this area
(3)(C) Appropriate DMHA roles for reserve components	No	Has not emerged as a priority issue
(3)(D) Information requirements, including advanced communications technology for virtual library	Yes	There is a need for developing/disseminating best practices on DoD responses to disasters, and maintaining a repository
(3)(E) Tropical medicine, particularly DoD medical readiness	No	Center for Disaster and Humanitarian Assistance Medicine (CDHAM), DoD surgeon general communities provide this
(4) Develop repository of disaster risk indicators for the Asia-Pacific region	No	PDC and academic institutions have developed indicators and are applying them globally to assess vulnerability
(5) Other missions as the Secretary of Defense may specify	Yes	CFE should maintain agility to undertake other high-priority DMHA-related missions "in CFE's lane" when gaps are identified

---

[2] The peacekeeping mission was included in the 2001 Defense Appropriations Act. It stated that CFE-DMHA "may also pay, or authorize payment for, the expenses of providing or facilitating education and training for appropriate military and civilian personnel of foreign countries in disaster management, peace operations, and humanitarian assistance." See Public Law 106-259, Department of Defense Appropriations Act, 2001, Section 8109, August 9, 2000.

agencies." Mission 1 is a generalized statement of the center's "bread and butter" and its niche—that of civ-mil coordination in DMHA across all types of humanitarian assistance scenarios.[3] CFE-DMHA continues to maintain leverage in the Asia-Pacific—through the use of its special authority to work with foreign civilian entities and its interagency coordinating role—in education and training, as well as engagement with foreign civilian and military organizations. As mentioned in Chapter Three, CFE-DMHA presents itself as the civilian face of DoD, making it easier for its interlocutors, including foreign-government civilian agencies and NGOs, to accept engagement with DoD; this has been greatly valued by PACOM and would also be of value in other theaters.[4] The center's staff helps maintain the necessary long-term relationships with DMHA stakeholders around the region and an understanding of the networks in which the international and NGO stakeholders operate. These engagements and relationships can help ensure that the education, training, and research that CFE-DMHA provides or facilitates are appropriate and relevant to a changing DMHA environment and that they address the needs and perspectives of the most-important U.S. and foreign stakeholders. CFE-DMHA is largely unique in DoD in its pursuit of this mission, and there continues to be a general need for these activities to enhance civ-mil coordination in humanitarian-assistance operations. CFE-DMHA's education and training efforts, including the HART, H.E.L.P., and UN-CMCoord courses, as well as its engagement activities with foreign entities, are extremely helpful at bringing U.S. military personnel and international partners together—and at helping the U.S. military bring its hierarchical command structure and capabilities to bear in the chaotic environment of disaster-relief operations. CFE-DMHA should provide its expertise and experience in bridging civilian and military efforts both to military DMHA operations and to the international humanitarian-assistance community.[5]

However, as indicated in Chapter Three, there is room for improvement in some of these activities, including research. National policy and strategy that define the role of the military in disasters will continue to evolve as new challenges emerge in disaster preparation and response, and CFE-DMHA should be at the cutting edge of formulating new concepts that may motivate necessary changes in policy. Responses by commanders will continue to be modified to fit the specific disaster in question and driven by direction from political authorities and the availability of resources. In one example specific to the PACOM AOR, although DMHA is a command priority (and a key Phase Zero activity[6]), PACOM planners maintain a planning assumption that deployed theater assets in DMHA missions will be "last in, first out."[7] This may fit the paradigm of natural disasters with a clear response phase, but each disaster is different and unpredictable. An Ebola-like infectious disease event in Asia, similar to the event in West Africa, may need a stronger and more sustained military presence, including medical intervention. These future contingency considerations all need careful thought; CFE-DMHA, in collaboration with academic or research institutions, could facilitate research efforts to address such fundamental questions and could focus on commonalities across disas-

---

[3]   Conversation with current or former CFE-DMHA staff, 2015.

[4]   Conversation with current or former PACOM officials, 2015; conversation with current or former HADR organization staff, 2015; conversations with current or former EUCOM and AFRICOM officials, 2015.

[5]   Conversation with current or former PACOM official, 2015.

[6]   Phase Zero refers to the "shaping" phase of DoD's operational planning construct.

[7]   Conversation with current or former CFE-DMHA staff, 2015.

ters, especially with regard to civ-mil coordination and associated processes. Accomplishing this will require the study and analysis of lessons learned and the development of a catalog of best practices, leading to the next mission that the center should continue pursuing. Emphasizing collaborative research as a CFE-DMHA core competency would hearken back to CFE-DMHA's original intended focus as a research organization that collaborates with academia on strategic-level DMHA challenges.

In addition, CFE-DMHA training efforts could be more tightly linked to the development and sustainment of long-term relationships if they emulated some practices of APCSS. APCSS nurtures its alumni networks, composed of former students from U.S. and foreign military and civilian organizations that participate in APCSS educational courses.[8] Prior RAND research on regional centers notes that the maintenance of strong alumni networks and frequent alumni outreach extends the influence that those centers have over time.[9] Outreach also provides entrée to senior partner-nation officials for U.S. policymakers and other USG officials. With appropriate resources (e.g., to maintain contact lists, disseminate information, and organize visits and events), outreach can pay off dramatically by facilitating surveys and information gathering (useful for assessing impact against specified metrics), by extending CFE-DMHA's ability to affect participants' activities long after the courses are over, and by providing greater access for the USG.[10] Finally, based on the analysis in Chapter Three, we conclude that, given the availability of PACOM resources and experience in planning and executing exercises, CFE-DMHA's involvement in this activity should be lessened to focus on assessing partner-nation DMHA capacity; capturing best practices; and coordinating with partner nations, international organizations, and NGOs.

"Mission (3)(D)—Provide and facilitate education, training, interagency coordination, and research on . . . [m]eeting requirements for information in connection with regional and global disasters, including the use of advanced communications technology as a virtual library." In our discussions with SMEs, we found broad agreement on the need for easy, rapid access to a broad array of information about DMHA, supported by increased emphasis on research and information sharing. Of greatest interest is an electronic repository of lessons learned and best practices for DoD disaster planning and response, something that does not exist. As noted in Chapter Three, CFE-DMHA products assessing foreign-nation disaster-response capabilities have been very well received. This is distinct from PDC's successful global efforts to use information technology for decision support during disasters and for the assessment of risk and vulnerability, which involves a different research focus. An expanded effort by CFE-DMHA to develop such a repository—and to populate it with best practices and lessons learned, some of which it integrates from existing studies or conducts alone or in concert with academic institutions—remains a critical CFE-DMHA mission. This effort should also facilitate the incorporation of the latest practices into CFE-DMHA and other education and training curricula.

Mission (5)—The Center shall perform such other missions as the Secretary of Defense may specify. As mentioned, while CFE-DMHA may not need to emphasize certain missions at this time, it should maintain the flexibility and agility to do so should it again be required by the Secretary of Defense. Likewise, the center should be prepared to contribute to missions

---

[8] Conversation with current or former CFE-DMHA staff, 2015.

[9] See Hanauer et al., 2014.

[10] Hanauer et al., 2014, pp. 85–92. Conversation with current or former CFE-DMHA staff, 2015.

not specified in the authority if the secretary determines the center to be the best-positioned organization to pursue them. Such missions could come in a number of different forms, such as those related to the impact climate change may have on certain Pacific Islands and densely populated coastal areas. Among the island states, aside from the potential shrinking of coastal areas (where most of the population resides), rising water levels may bring high levels of salinity to underground fresh water supplies. DMHA takes on new meaning when one considers the contingency to evacuate entire populations. The Secretary of Defense might consider whether CFE-DMHA, perhaps in concert with other USG organizations, such as the National Oceanic and Atmospheric Administration (NOAA), should explore the impact of climate change and think about the role of military forces in future disaster scenarios.

The center, however, must forge a balance among maintaining agility, taking on high-priority missions approved by the secretary, and focusing on its traditional efforts. "Other missions as assigned" can lead to the "mission creep" that dilutes CFE-DMHA's focus and diminishes its ability to be effective in its core missions. It would be prudent to ensure that any guidance regarding future disaster scenarios comes with dedicated resources for the additional missions or, if resources are not provided, that guidance specifies activities CFE-DMHA should deemphasize to take on new missions.

Missions CFE-DMHA Can Deemphasize in the Near Term

"Mission (2)—The Center shall be used to make available high-quality disaster management and humanitarian assistance in response to disasters." Generally, CFE-DMHA has shed the response mission because of its small size and the fact that numerous other organizations—civilian and military, foreign and domestic—now conduct exercises to practice disaster response, respond to disasters, and manage their consequences. U.S. military organizations, especially PACOM, "lean forward" to be ready to respond, if requested, more systematically than was the case in 1994.

There are three areas in which CFE-DMHA might continue to participate in a response role, and thus we suggest in Table 4.1 that the mission overall be partially emphasized. The first is in providing advice to the geographic combatant commander or the commander of a joint task force, if one is established for a particular disaster. A CFE-DMHA advisor could be pulled from the staff during contingencies based on his or her experience in previous exercises and disasters and expertise built through the pursuit of other Title 10 missions and supporting activities. Second, as part of its research activities to develop best practices, CFE-DMHA and other experts should be on the ground early during a major disaster to assemble lessons learned and add to the information contained in the virtual library or repository. Fieldwork must be a critical part of research into fundamental questions of roles and the establishment of best practices based on developing a common picture of disaster response and post-disaster consequence management, where the military is a contributing participant. This is especially important because CFE-DMHA is getting better at fieldwork, following the mixed results of the Haiyan lessons learned. Finally, CFE-DMHA has proven to be an effective transmitter of information and situational awareness between international organizations and the U.S. military during crises.[11] This is a natural role stemming from CFE-DMHA's establishment of long-

---

[11] For example, during Typhoon Hagupit in the Philippines, CFE-DMHA provided OCHA with timely information about the U.S. military response. As a result of this and other cooperative efforts, OCHA Bangkok favors CFE-DMHA

term relationships with humanitarian-assistance stakeholders. We conclude that CFE-DMHA could continue its indirect role in disaster response and defer its direct role in this mission.

"Mission (3)(A)—Provide and facilitate education, training, interagency coordination, and research on . . . [m]anagement of the consequences of nuclear, biological, and chemical events." CFE-DMHA recently set aside its role in CBRN consequence management, which makes sense given the other organizations in the field. DTRA is a DoD resource on operational training for foreign consequence management in coordination with the CCMDs and deploys training teams to selected foreign countries. DTRA engages DoD's regional centers to provide chemical- and biological-warfare consequence management to partner-nation officials.[12] Although DTRA does not have a mandate for medical training, part of foreign consequence management training is to provide standards for medical response. DTRA is also the operational component of the Cooperative Biological Engagement Program (CBEP). Although largely a surveillance and safety program for controlling extremely dangerous pathogens in foreign countries, CBEP is targeted at preventing bioweapon development and use.[13] In addition, Congress provided funding to the Center for Disaster and Humanitarian Assistance Medicine (CDHAM) to develop first-responder training on CBRN response. While that funding has expired, the precedent remains. CDHAM is also DTRA's medical partner for CBEP.[14]

The reserve components have also established CBRN hazard-response teams that support FEMA. These teams are FEMA trained and DoD equipped, are deployable, and serve all 50 states and U.S. territories. The U.S. Marine Corps created its own Chemical Biological Incident Response Force (CBIRF). CBIRF deploys or responds to a CBRN threat or event to assist local, state, or federal agencies and the geographic combatant commanders. It provides capabilities for command and control; agent detection and identification; search, rescue, and decontamination; and emergency medical care for contaminated personnel. This team receives FEMA, DoD, and service training and trains other Marines and select personnel from other organizations.[15] The existence of CBRN training and response capabilities at DTRA, the reserve components, and the Marine Corps means that CFE-DMHA is neither unique nor best positioned to pursue CBRN as a mission at this time.

"Mission (3)(B)—Provide and facilitate education, training, interagency coordination, and research on . . . [m]anagement of the consequences of terrorism." The growth since the attacks of September 11, 2001, in the number of organizations with expertise in counterterrorism and associated consequence management has been exponential. Foreign and domestic law-enforcement agencies and military organizations have gained expertise in terrorism-related issues and developed experience in working collaboratively to prevent, prepare for, and mitigate the consequences of terrorist attacks. Some DMHA organizations have also built terrorism-related expertise in their focus areas, including CDHAM, whose portfolio includes the med-

---

participation in its international response team when disaster strikes. An international organization requesting such a contribution from a DoD organization is quite unusual. Conversation with current or former CFE-DMHA staff, 2015.

[12] Hanauer et al., 2014, p. 67.

[13] Phone conversation with current or former PACOM officials, 2015.

[14] Conversation with current or former HADR organization staff, 2015.

[15] "Chemical Biological Incident Response Force," U.S. Marine Corps, undated.

ical aspect of responses to terrorist events.[16] Thus, CFE-DMHA's particular involvement in this mission at this time appears superfluous.

"Mission (3)(C)—Provide and facilitate education, training, interagency coordination, and research on . . . [a]ppropriate roles for the reserve components in the management of such consequences and in disaster management and humanitarian assistance in response to natural disasters." In general, expanding the understanding of the role of the reserve components (the National Guard and the Reserves) in DMHA does not appear to be a current need for CFE-DMHA. In fact, the National Guard has improved its training and response capacity over the past 20 years, and its members have relevant expertise from their professional roles in civilian life. Domestically, FEMA created the Incident Management and Coordination System (part of the National Response Framework) after Hurricane Katrina, which involves the National Guard in its Title 32 role. Since FEMA approaches disasters from an "all hazards" perspective, the members of the military, by virtue of their uniformed specialties, are part of Support to Civil Authorities and receive education and training that encompass all the missions listed above. For example, in addition to any military training at the major command level, the reserve components are trained in the same manner as civilian responders. Often, reservists gain skills relevant to disaster response in their civilian jobs and may themselves be first responders to disasters in the United States. Under the National Guard State Partnership Program, members of the Guard, in their Title 10 role, participate with partner countries in annual training events that include many DMHA activities. Currently, there are 68 unique security partnerships, involving 74 nations around the globe.

"Mission (3)(E)—Provide and facilitate education, training, interagency coordination, and research on . . . [t]ropical medicine, particularly in relation to the medical readiness requirements of the Department of Defense." This mission has been more broadly interpreted to include infectious diseases, helping lead to CFE-DMHA's foray into HIV/AIDS work in the early 2000s. CDHAM appears to accomplish this mission globally, including in the Asia-Pacific. On the basis of a congressional mandate, the Uniformed Services University of the Health Sciences established CDHAM in 1999 as an academic resource for DoD, in the areas of humanitarian assistance and disaster-response medicine. This resource is further defined as providing support to DoD agencies through education, training, consultation, scholarly activities, and direct support regarding health care in response to disasters and in humanitarian-assistance missions. CDHAM claims to be the focal point and academic center in the military health system for liaison to various governmental, nongovernmental, and international organizations (such as the World Health Organization and the Pan American Health Organization). CDHAM works closely with CCMDs to pursue its education and training mission. It performs tasks in the Asia-Pacific region, at times in cooperation with CFE-DMHA under a 2007 MOU. CDHAM teaches and trains on measures of effectiveness, metrics, and evaluations for global health engagement. The CDHAM mandate was strengthened under the Obama administration, when the Assistant Secretary of Defense for Health Affairs made health engagement (sometimes called health diplomacy) a high priority.[17]

As indicated above, deemphasizing CFE-DMHA's role in a mission does not preclude activities that may contribute in important ways to specific types of disasters. The Ebola out-

[16] Conversation with current or former HADR organization staff, 2015.

[17] Conversation with current or former HADR organization staff, 2015.

break in West Africa in 2014 is a case in point. CFE-DMHA training on civ-mil coordination (i.e., the HART course) could have helped U.S. military units that responded to the outbreak in Liberia, when they arrived in Monrovia, to understand what to expect in dealing with multiple national and international organizations. Such preparation, while not necessarily particular to a disaster involving infectious disease, could reduce confusion in the early days of a disaster and help military responders have a more immediate impact on efforts to relieve suffering. As suggested, CFE-DMHA SMEs could provide insights from best practices to OSD and the combatant commander as they plan a response.

"Mission (4) The Center shall develop a repository of disaster risk indicators for the Asia-Pacific region." Finally, the development and dissemination of risk and vulnerability indicators has been an important role for the mostly DoD-funded PDC, both in the Asia-Pacific region and globally. Advances in information technology and awareness of risk management have enabled PDC to create emergency-preparedness tools since its establishment in 1998. Its core competencies are multihazard warning and decision-support applications, as well as risk and vulnerability methods to assess resilience and coping capacity at the global, national, and subnational levels (some of which feed decision-support applications). PDC uses information, science, and technology to promote disaster-risk reduction concepts and strategies. PDC also conducts risk assessments that integrate hazard exposure with socioeconomic factors and does training, workshops, and exercises in disaster management that focus on how to use PDC's free tools (DisasterAWARE and Emergency Operations [EMOPS]).[18]

In sum, given the existence of multiple organizations on the DMHA landscape with overlapping authorities, we do not find that CFE-DMHA should equally emphasize all of its Title 10 missions at this time, and we have identified a subset of missions that are most relevant for CFE-DMHA to pursue. CFE-DMHA continues to provide DoD with leverage in key DMHA missions authorized by Congress. We now turn to the question of where CFE-DMHA should pursue activities to carry out these missions.

CFE-DMHA's Missions Need to Be Addressed Globally

In Title 10, Section 182, Congress assigned missions to CFE-DMHA with the intention that they should be carried out globally (with the exception of the repository of disaster-risk indicators, where the Asia-Pacific focus is specified). Indeed, while the Asia-Pacific region is the single-most disaster-prone region for both natural and technological disasters, some 55 percent of disasters since 1990 have occurred in other regions, such as Africa, Europe, and South America. Moreover, the frequency in these other regions of natural disasters between 2000 and 2010 increased by 43 percent, compared with the previous decade, while in the Asia-Pacific it increased 36 percent. And while the vast majority of deaths have occurred in disasters in the Asia-Pacific, almost half of the economic damage, valued at about $845 billion, has been suffered in other regions.[19] Thus, the global nature of the challenge in preparing for, responding to, and mitigating the effects of disasters is not in doubt.

---

[18] Conversation with current or former HADR organization staff, 2015.

[19] See EM-DAT: The International Disaster Database (www.emdat.be), which is available from the Centre for Research on the Epidemiology of Disasters, Université Catholique de Louvain, Brussels (figures as of August 2015).

RAND discussions with multiple organizations and experts, as well as our document review, corroborate the need for an organization with a truly global outlook that advances civ-mil coordination in DMHA and that helps meet requirements that are not being met at this time. Despite forays into other theaters, CFE-DMHA has not had much success beyond the Asia-Pacific region. It continues to be viewed as a "PACOM asset" for several reasons: it was established by Senator Inouye, it is located in Hawaii, PACOM has had operational control "from the beginning," and it has had no permanent representation outside the theater.[20] Disasters are more numerous and frequent in the PACOM AOR, and it is there where the U.S. military is most likely to be asked to respond. Nevertheless, there are broader needs that require CFE-DMHA's Title 10 authority to be met globally. Orienting CFE-DMHA globally would require resources that have not been available to it, as well as a reconfiguration of its current organizational structure. We discuss these issues below, in the section on courses of action.

The RAND study team held focused discussions with several current and former officials, as well as contracted personnel, from each of the CCMDs and from OSD to identify critical requirements to effectively execute DMHA programs. While we approached a relatively small number of discussants, they had deep experience planning and managing theater and global efforts in DMHA and represented an important cross-section of expertise in this area. The common challenges they identified are not necessarily ongoing deficiencies, as some CCMDs have developed or are planning to develop capabilities to address them. These common challenges revolved around (1) a lack of coherent management of DMHA issues; (2) inadequate education, training, and experience among command staff and responding units; and (3) a lack of ready access to analytical products, including country-baseline assessments or databases of lessons learned or best practices. A fourth challenge—inadequate consideration of DMHA in CCMD theater campaign planning and exercises—appeared to be of less concern.

Dispersed Management and Low Prioritization of the Enterprise

Each CCMD is responsible for conducting a broad range of DMHA activities that require engaging an equally broad set of stakeholders as well as marshaling a diverse set of capabilities. At the same time, some CCMDs (e.g., CENTCOM) are faced with even more-daunting and immediate operational challenges, such as the fight against the Islamic State, that can over-shadow humanitarian-assistance planning and execution and relegate them to a lower priority. The crucial task for CCMDs is to coordinate a diverse set of interagency partners, foreign governments and militaries, and nongovernmental and international organizations in managing HADR missions and responsibilities. Each CCMD has developed a unique framework for addressing these issues that, in varying degrees, is disaggregated among several entities or directorates across the CCMD staff, making coordinated efforts more difficult and complex. But several discussants noted that in most commands there is no flag officer–level champion of disaster preparedness in theater and no systematic strategy to implement DMHA efforts (PACOM and SOUTHCOM were exceptions). This was cited as an important gap.[21]

In some commands, the responsibility for planning, programming, and coordinating DMHA efforts is dispersed across several directorates, diluting the focus and effectiveness of those efforts. EUCOM has divided its humanitarian-assistance and disaster-relief responsi-

---

[20] Phone conversation with current or former CFE-DMHA staff, 2014; and conversations with multiple experts, 2014–2015.

[21] Phone conversations with current or former EUCOM, AFRICOM, and CENTCOM officials, 2015.

bilities among its J4 Logistics Directorate, responsible for OHDACA-funded disaster-relief programs and some Humanitarian Civil Assistance programs; the J5/8, Policy, Strategy and Partnering Capabilities Directorate, which manages disaster-reduction and -mitigation programs; and the J9 directorate, which oversees interagency partnering and works primarily with USAID and OFDA to support HADR activities.[22] CENTCOM manages its responsibilities more centrally, through its HADR, Disaster Relief and Mine Action (HDM) office in the J3 Operations Directorate and focuses primarily on OHDACA-funded programs.[23] The command relies on civil-affairs personnel to conduct steady-state DMHA activities within subordinate commands, but there is no coordinating function at the CENTCOM staff level to synchronize or deconflict humanitarian assistance–related civil-affairs activities in theater.[24] AFRICOM's activities had been centered in the eight-person Humanitarian and Health Activities cell until recently, but this office was abolished and its personnel scattered across the staff, leaving one official (occasionally supplemented by a reservist) to manage AFRICOM's HADR programming.[25] PACOM's J3, J4, J5, and J9 directorates all have responsibility for various aspects of DMHA.

NORTHCOM, with primary responsibility for homeland security and defense, does not have as extensive a foreign DMHA portfolio as other geographic CCMDs. Accordingly, its program office is located within the J9 Interagency Coordination Directorate and has responsibility for disaster preparedness and disaster relief; disaster response is assigned as a J3 Operations responsibility.[26]

Mainly because of SOUTHCOM's primary focus on engagement activities, humanitarian-assistance and disaster-relief issues tend to be more prevalent and have higher priority for it than for other CCMDs. Only SOUTHCOM has made a deliberate effort to consolidate DMHA missions and responsibilities under a single division.[27] Under the J7 Interagency Engagement Directorate, the J74 Civil-Military Assistance Division focuses on coordinating engagement within partner nations to close capability gaps; develop policy guidance and funding issues for disaster response; and oversee all education, medical, and basic infrastructure projects in the region.[28]

PACOM has made CFE-DMHA the coordinating entity for disparate DMHA issues within the command.[29] More recently, PACOM established an Inter-Agency Coordination Directorate (J9), with the subordinate J91 All-Hazards office, which oversees the command's humanitarian-assistance activities. Because of conflicting guidance, it too has begun to assume more coordination and collaboration responsibilities.[30] However, as one official noted, without clearer guidance delineating responsibilities between the PACOM J9 and CFE-DMHA,

---

[22] Phone conversation with current or former EUCOM officials, 2015.

[23] DSCA overseas OHDACA funding, which is used to fund DoD programs that address partner-nation capability gaps and disaster-relief operations. Phone conversation with current or former CENTCOM officials, 2015.

[24] Phone conversation with current or former CENTCOM official, 2015.

[25] Phone conversations with current or former AFRICOM officials, 2015.

[26] Phone conversation with current or former NORTHCOM officials, 2015.

[27] Phone conversation with current or former SOUTHCOM official, 2015.

[28] Phone conversation with current or former SOUTHCOM official, 2015.

[29] PACOM, 2013.

[30] Conversation with current or former PACOM official, 2015.

DoD does not speak with a unified voice to partner nations and other stakeholders in the Asia-Pacific region.[31]

While a globally oriented CFE-DMHA building a positive reputation may not be a panacea for the distributed DMHA responsibilities and low priority accorded to the mission area in many commands—or replace relevant staff functions—it could serve over time as an advocate to combatant commanders for disaster-management efforts. CFE-DMHA representatives or liaisons placed on command staffs (see the courses of action below) would be better able to support civ-mil coordination efforts in theater and pursue advocacy from within the command. However, simply asserting that CFE-DMHA has a global mission does not guarantee buy-in for this concept by the CCMDs. The CCMDs (except PACOM) would need to be convinced of the benefits CFE-DMHA could offer for achieving their own objectives and lines of effort, as well of the utility of CFE-DMHA as a source of DMHA expertise for CCMD staff. Moreover, caution would be warranted in the roles that CFE-DMHA experts or liaisons would play to avoid the perception that they are "extra bodies" available to the CCMD staff to meet internal command staff responsibilities. Careful deconfliction of roles of CFE-DMHA experts and CCMD staffs would be warranted.

Insufficiently Trained and Experienced Managers and Responding Forces
In addressing humanitarian-assistance issues, DoD faces a continuing challenge in maintaining a workforce of well-trained and experienced individuals. Like warfighting functions, the need for DMHA training and education is not static and will be in continuous demand at all stages of a military career. For the CCMDs, this includes maintaining such individuals, both on their staffs and among units that respond to disasters within their theaters, who understand and can operate within a civ-mil DMHA environment. For the most part, humanitarian assistance is not a core competency for military personnel (neither is it a "primary mission" for DoD) and typically is prioritized lower than competing mission areas, resulting in shortfalls of DMHA-experienced military personnel.[32] Moreover, the chaotic command-and-control environment of disasters (with multiple U.S. and host-nation government agencies, international organizations, NGOs, and local stakeholders involved in the same operating space) stands in stark contrast to the highly structured, hierarchical command system that U.S. military members have internalized. Military work and management in the DMHA environment requires training and experience.

While many discussants commented on specific training requirements for particular CCMDs, there was general consensus that DMHA personnel lack sufficient training and experience, especially in understanding how the USG will respond to a foreign disaster. One discussant remarked that many disaster-management personnel, including senior leadership, have not attended OFDA's JHOC, which can result in the development of unclear or conflicting guidance for staff planners.[33] EUCOM officials have also noted a lack of disaster-management expe-

---

[31] Conversation with current or former PACOM official, 2015.

[32] Yet "conduct humanitarian assistance and disaster response" was mentioned as one of the 12 joint force prioritized missions in the 2015 National Military Strategy (DoD, *The National Military Strategy of the United States of America 2015*, Washington, D.C., June 2015, p. 11).

[33] Phone conversation with current or former NORTHCOM officials, 2015.

rience among many action officers reporting to the staff.[34] Within EUCOM, the branch chief responsible for managing disaster-preparedness programs has been gapped for nearly a year; previously, the position was filled by a government civilian, and then temporarily by a reservist.[35] EUCOM also lacks an adequate number of dedicated personnel to oversee disaster-management programs and has sought to supplement its staff through the State Partnership Program with National Guard personnel who have disaster-management expertise.[36] The PACOM J3 Operations Directorate, with oversight of disaster-response operations, does not have the requisite experience to handle DMHA planning, relying instead on CFE-DMHA to provide expertise and knowledge for improving how interagency organizations coordinate assistance and response operations.[37]

Training and experience in DMHA is not only a requirement for the CCMD staffs but also for forces reporting to a region. Because of the focus on combat operations within CENTCOM, training in DMHA for personnel deployed to the region, primarily Special Operations Central Command (SOCCENT) and, to a lesser extent, civil-affairs personnel from the Army Central Command (ARCENT), is prioritized lower than other warfighting capabilities.[38] CENTCOM has delegated responsibility to the components providing response forces or the joint task force commander receiving these units to ensure that the forces have the proper training; CENTCOM staff provides little oversight regarding the type or quality of training.[39] One interlocutor remarked that most units and staff in the AFRICOM AOR, including most civil-affairs personnel, have little or no DMHA training, and that their participation in disaster response (e.g., the Ebola crisis) was often a "one-off" experience.[40]

While education is important, high turnover rates among military personnel, as well as government civilians, at overseas CCMDs (EUCOM, AFRICOM, and parts of CENTCOM) cause discontinuities in operational ability because of the loss of institutional knowledge and of long-established relationships with partner nations. CCMDs must be able to establish and maintain long-term relationships with the humanitarian-assistance community so as to better plan and execute humanitarian-assistance missions. While several CCMDs use National Guard units to provide longevity and institutional knowledge, this does not offset losses, because of active-duty and civilian staff turnover.[41]

SOUTHCOM may be an outlier regarding command focus and staff training for DMHA. SOUTHCOM has focused on building an experienced civilian workforce to execute related programs, that now include 18 active-duty, reservist, and government civilian personnel. This staff comprises acquisition specialists, a training specialist, operations specialists, and budgeteers to facilitate building partner capacity and internal resilience to natural disasters.[42]

---

[34] Phone conversation with current or former EUCOM officials, 2015.

[35] Phone conversation with current or former EUCOM officials, 2015.

[36] Phone conversation with current or former EUCOM officials, 2015.

[37] Conversation with current or former PACOM officials, 2015.

[38] Phone conversation with current or former CENTCOM officials, 2015.

[39] Phone conversation with current or former CENTCOM officials, 2015.

[40] Phone conversation with current or former AFRICOM officials, 2015.

[41] Phone conversation with current or former EUCOM officials, 2015.

[42] Phone conversation with current or former SOUTHCOM officials, 2015.

The command has also developed battle staff plans for additional personnel support required from stakeholder organizations in disaster-response efforts.[43] SOUTHCOM strives to maintain a maximum number of personnel current in the JHOC. To do so, it sends staff action officers to regional embassies to receive the training with the security cooperation officer, who is the primary interlocutor between DoD efforts and foreign military and civilian agencies handling DMHA activities within the country.[44] SOUTHCOM supplements JHOC training by contracting with one of six licensed and certified vendors in its Indefinite Duration Indefinite Quality contracting program to deliver additional disaster-management training to staff personnel.[45]

A number of current and former OSD officials with DMHA-related portfolios concurred that there is insufficient training and experience for staff and responding forces.[46] Some noted, for example, that the effectiveness of DoD's response to the 2014 Ebola outbreak in West Africa was impeded because the "civ-mil coordination did not work well," and there was little relevant preparation for civ-mil coordination challenges.[47] OSD officials have expressed a desire for "institutionalizing HADR training" globally. A reconfigured CFE-DMHA could be a part of this effort through expansion of its HART course and related training and education efforts. As mentioned in Chapter Three, the HART course is designed to help military members (and students from other organizations, foreign and domestic) understand what to expect when they arrive at a disaster. This is training that the JHOC—which focuses on policies, authorities, and lines of command in a U.S. response to disasters—does not provide.[48] Disaster-management training on civ-mil coordination is relevant across disasters and regions but would be strengthened by information about regional humanitarian-assistance networks.

Limited Access to Authoritative Analytical Products and Lessons Learned
The limited number of DMHA-dedicated personnel assigned to CCMD staffs has oversight over a broad scope of activities. Planning and execution typically takes precedence over analysis and assessments. As a result, DMHA planning is sometimes based on informal or narrowly scoped analysis, conducted by personnel with limited experience or expertise or by outside organizations that are not necessarily tailored to the requirements of the particular CCMD. EUCOM, for example, requires country-baseline assessments to identify capability gaps and help focus resources to partner nations. It lacks, however, an inherent ability to assess partner-nation capabilities, instead relying on the Defense Threat Reduction Agency for assessment products, or State Partnership Program personnel for institutional knowledge in developing analytical requirements for the J5 Directorate.[49] Complicating the issue in EUCOM is the lack of country-level assessments from Security Cooperation Officers in the region, where disaster preparation is only a small portion of their responsibilities. Consequently, there is little time

---

[43] Phone conversation with current or former SOUTHCOM officials, 2015.

[44] Phone conversation with current or former SOUTHCOM officials, 2015.

[45] Phone conversation with current or former SOUTHCOM officials, 2015.

[46] Multiple conversations with current or former DoD officials, 2014–2015.

[47] Conversation with current or former DoD officials, 2015.

[48] Multiple conversations with current or former CCMD, OSD, and CFE-DMHA officials, 2014–2015; phone conversation with current or former USAID official, 2015.

[49] Phone conversation with current or former EUCOM officials, 2015.

for security cooperation officers to dedicate to disaster preparation assessments.[50] CENTCOM also has limited capability to produce assessments. Its HDM office does not have the manpower to work with other organizations, such as OFDA, to obtain assessments that could inform its planning processes. Consequently, it has little ability to provide leadership with a comprehensive picture of the DMHA environment in country.[51]

Some CCMDs, such as PACOM's J9 Pacific Outreach Directorate, have established specialized relationships with outside organizations to develop tailored analytical products. Lacking sufficient internal subject-matter expertise and commensurate analytical capability for planning purposes, PACOM has partnered with CFE-DMHA to provide this analysis. This has included development of a white paper on the impact of El Niño on weather-related security contingencies, country books annotating national DMHA capabilities and shortfalls, and other products that can inform strategic and operational planning. PACOM has also worked with CFE-DMHA to synthesize Department of State strategies with other stakeholders, such as USAID and the UN, to provide an analytic product informing PACOM's strategic planning over a five-year period.[52] AFRICOM relies on CDHAM to develop baseline country capability analyses for building health and disaster response capacity in a small number of African nations.[53]

In contrast to the other CCMDs, both NORTHCOM and SOUTHCOM rely on internal analysis and assessment capabilities, although these vary in their effectiveness. Still, both commands need to supplement internal capability with outside expertise. SOUTHCOM contracts some analysis with outside organizations, including PDC and OCHA, to develop country baseline assessments and measures of effectiveness and performance to determine a level of achievement in narrowing capability gaps.[54] NORTHCOM has partnered with PDC to provide risk identification, vulnerability analysis, and lessons learned, in conjunction with DMHA programs.[55]

In addition to analytical products, many discussants noted that a comprehensive source of lessons learned and best practices would benefit DMHA planning and execution, as most such issues are generic and can easily apply across disaster types and geographic boundaries.[56] NORTHCOM does not develop lessons learned internally but collects them from interagency organizations or exterior partners, including information sharing with SOUTHCOM.[57] Such lessons learned, however, are "more relevant to the customer" in partner nations than to NORTHCOM staff.[58] CENTCOM's HDM office is able to develop assessments by culling from various sources that are only indirectly relevant to DMHA—e.g., lessons learned from the Joint Lessons Learned Information System, Civil Military Support Element reports, USAID,

---

[50] Phone conversation with current or former EUCOM officials, 2015.

[51] Phone conversation with current or former CENTCOM official, 2015.

[52] Conversation with current or former PACOM official, 2015.

[53] Phone conversation with current or former AFRICOM official, 2015.

[54] Phone conversation with current or former SOUTHCOM official, 2015.

[55] Phone conversation with current or former NORTHCOM official, 2015.

[56] Multiple conversations with current or former CCMD and other DoD officials, 2014–2015.

[57] Phone conversation with current or former NORTHCOM official, 2015.

[58] Phone conversation with current or former NORTHCOM official, 2015.

and the State Department.[59] One discussant noted that the HDM office could better support command activities and inform planning processes if it had access to better data regarding DMHA activities in theater, including locations of nongovernmental and international organizations working within the region or countries and the activities they are conducting.[60]

PACOM has developed a framework to help allocate limited resources and develop milestones to achieve strategic objectives within each country. This framework, however, requires a comprehensive baseline assessment of each country, including capabilities and gaps, to better understand the starting point for developing milestones and events.[61] The lack of a consolidated database of DMHA lessons learned is also seen as a gap. One discussant noted the value that would accrue to the CCMDs by capturing lessons learned from the Ebola response regarding the dynamics between various organizations operating in West Africa.[62] A global central repository of lessons learned would help mitigate the loss of institutional knowledge because of personnel turnover.[63]

The RAND team found very broad agreement among interlocutors on the need for a central repository of lessons learned and best practices. Most CCMDs also expressed a need for country assessments and other analytic products. A reconfigured CFE-DMHA could provide such a repository, supported by research efforts to systematically develop best practices in DMHA.

To Pursue Its Missions Globally, a Recast CFE-DMHA Should Merge with a Globally Oriented DoD Organization

We have identified several key Title 10 missions and associated activities assigned to CFE-DMHA that should continue to be filled by a dedicated DoD organization. We have demonstrated that elements of an enduring need for these missions exist not only in the Asia-Pacific region but in other theaters as well. If CFE-DMHA is to fulfill these needs, it will need to be reconfigured and given appropriate guidance, resources, and structure. As one interlocutor asked, "Can an organization smaller than an army platoon accomplish a global mission? I don't think so."[64]

What form should a reconfigured CFE-DMHA take? This section reviews some courses of action (COAs) that would define a future configuration for CFE-DMHA. Our research suggests that a merger with an existing, globally oriented DoD organization would provide the course of action most likely to ensure CFE-DMHA's success in accomplishing its global missions and in enhancing its reputation for excellence, as well as in serving as a reliable partner in DMHA.

There are many COAs that OSD might consider for a reconfigured CFE-DMHA. We consider five that, with appropriate focus and resources, could help improve the effectiveness

---

[59] Phone conversation with current or former CENTCOM official, 2015.

[60] Phone conversation with current or former CENTCOM official, 2015.

[61] Conversation with current or former PACOM official, 2015.

[62] Conversation with current or former PACOM officials, 2015.

[63] Conversation with current or former OSD officials, 2015.

[64] Phone conversation with current or former CFE-DMHA staff, 2015.

and efficiency of DoD's civ-mil coordination efforts in DMHA in the Asia-Pacific region and globally. We differentiate the COAs by the focus of the organization or center that follows the current CFE-DMHA—i.e., whether the center is focused only on DMHA civ-mil coordination in the Asia-Pacific region or on global needs. We assume that any COA executed would incorporate the attributes of a healthy organization (adequate guidance and resources, assessment process, proper mission support functions, etc.), outlined at the end of Chapter Three.

Table 4.2 displays the five COAs we considered. The columns represent the source of core funding for each COA (at least initially) and the geographic orientation associated with it.

The COAs we considered are as follows.

- *COA 1: Absorption by PACOM.* The CFE-DMHA's capability would be wholly absorbed under a directorate on the PACOM staff. This COA would result in CFE-DMHA focusing solely on the Asia-Pacific region. It would entail incorporation of administrative functions into the command and transfer of the center's USG billets to the PACOM staff. Activities would be wholly aligned with the PACOM directorate under which the capability resides but could continue to include support to engagements and exercises, the command's crisis response, analysis of partner disaster-response capabilities in the AOR, and other requirements that the PACOM commander and staff director set. Absorption of CFE-DMHA into the PACOM staff would eliminate the existence of CFE-DMHA's current "civilian face," which many interlocutors had noted is often advantageous in dealing with partner nations, international organizations, and NGOs.
- *COA 2: Absorption by Asia-Pacific–focused organization.* The CFE-DMHA's capability would be wholly incorporated under the director of an Asia-Pacific–oriented DoD civilian organization, such as APCSS. Absorption by PDC, also in Hawaii, is another possibility, although PDC has global focus and presence and is considered in COA 5. CFE-DMHA could remain a separate center with an executive who reports to the director of the larger host organization. Core funding would be provided by DSCA, and administrative and overhead functions would be undertaken by the host organization. CFE-DMHA would continue to conduct DMHA education and training, regional engagements, and analysis of partner DMHA capabilities and lessons learned in conjunction with other partners, such as the University of Hawaii.

Table 4.2
Courses of Action Considered for a Reconfigured CFE-DMHA

Course of Action	Core Funding Source	Asia-Pacific Regional Orientation	Global Orientation
1. Absorption by PACOM	Navy O&M	√	
2. Absorption by Asia-Pacific–focused organization	OSD/DSCA	√	
3. PACOM DRU (current status)	Navy O&M	√	
4. Stand-alone organization	OSD/DSCA		√
5. Absorption by globally focused organization	OSD/DSCA		√

- *COA 3: PACOM DRU.* CFE-DMHA would remain a direct reporting unit to PACOM, and thus focused solely on the Asia-Pacific region, but would be positioned and resourced to effectively pursue the Title 10 missions defined earlier in this chapter. CFE-DMHA would focus its efforts on regional engagements, education and training, information sharing, and advising but would shed its global mission. It would still need to be right-sized and funded to its regional functions, and the right mix of USG and contract employees would have to be executed. This would have to be accompanied by robust guidance from PACOM to increase CFE-DMHA's effectiveness in the Asia-Pacific.
- *COA 4: Stand-alone organization.* CFE-DMHA would become a center with OSD oversight and funded through DSCA, but with a focus that is global. With a global focus, a stand-alone organization would work with OSD to set its global priorities, as well as with the CCMDs to define and prioritize CFE-DMHA goals and activities in different regions. In this case, CFE-DMHA would be akin to an independent functional center, in contrast to DoD's regional centers, which it would most definitely *not* be designed to replace. These regional centers (such as APCSS in PACOM's AOR and the Marshall Center in EUCOM's) are critical to regional engagement and building and maintaining relationships with particular countries and cultural milieus.[65] More appropriately, CFE-DMHA and regional centers should leverage each other's comparative advantages to enhance their own mission areas (as CFE-DMHA and APCSS do now, at least nominally).
- *COA 5: Absorption by a globally focused organization.* CFE-DMHA would be wholly incorporated under the director of a globally oriented DoD civilian organization; an example might be CCMR or even PDC. However, this COA would also incorporate regional aspects of coordination and support. CFE-DMHA would constitute a center under the host-organization director and would be core funded by DSCA, with oversight and guidance from OSD, perhaps through a dedicated principal deputy assistant secretary of defense board akin to the one that meets semiannually to provide integrated, senior-level guidance to the regional centers.[66] OSD guidance would incorporate and prioritize CCMD requirements. The center would retain a core of DMHA expertise in the continental United States (CONUS), and would provide liaisons to the CCMDs with reachback to expertise in CONUS. The liaisons would support CCMD objectives by providing advice, visibility into theater needs, support for DMHA civ-mil coordination and activities, and advocacy of CFE-DMHA as a resource. To help ensure continued support to the Asia-Pacific and PACOM, there would be a significantly reinforced CFE-DMHA presence in that theater, particularly in the initial stages of COA 5 execution.

A COA that associates CFE-DMHA with an Asia-Pacific–oriented organization (whether PACOM or other Pacific-focused DoD entities) would not enable the center to adequately fulfill global missions. This is an important assumption that is based on CFE-DMHA's history and multiple conversations across the spectrum of DoD organizations that the RAND team engaged. Despite efforts to meet global requirements since 2000, CFE-DMHA has naturally been engulfed by the requirements and priorities of PACOM, which provides CFE-DMHA's funding and oversees its functioning, including appointing its director, who reports to the

---

[65] See Hanauer et al., 2014, pp. 125–127.

[66] Hanauer et al., 2014, p. xiii.

commander directly or through the chief of staff and vice commander. The notion of OSD oversight, which has often been vague and sporadic, partly because of the lack of financial control, does not change the fact that it has been mostly perceived by potential extraregional customers (e.g., other CCMDs) as a "PACOM asset." If CFE were to align with another regionally focused organization, it is reasonable to assume that the regional priorities of the host organization would dominate CFE-DMHA's agenda and that other CCMDs and organizations focused on other theaters would not view CFE-DMHA as an enduring asset. However, this does not preclude a regionally oriented CFE-DMHA resourced to strengthen its education and training, knowledge management, and research initiatives from making available to other CCMDs and extraregional stakeholders its "exportable" repository of best practices and online courses, which would come at little cost to CFE-DMHA or the customers. At the same time, it should be noted that a center focused only on one region would be cheaper than one with a global orientation; thus, a decision to create a global CFE-DMHA is dependent on the availability of funds to do so.

Given our conclusion that a recast CFE-DMHA should have a global orientation, we focus our analysis on the two globally oriented COAs—4 and 5. Table 4.3 provides a comparison of the unique strengths and weaknesses of the two COAs and offers an order-of-magnitude estimate of the resources needed to operate the center and fund its activities.

Table 4.3
Strengths and Weaknesses of Two Globally Oriented Courses of Action

Qualities	COA 4: Stand-Alone Organization	COA 5: Absorption by Globally Oriented Organization
Unique strengths	• Competition for resources directly tied to OSD and CCMD requirements • Minimizes bureaucratic layers between CFE-DMHA and oversight/guidance	• Enables CFE-DMHA to associate reputation with that of host organization • CFE-DMHA could build on host-organization stakeholder networks in other theaters • CFE-DMHA activities could be incorporated into existing host-organization assessment processes • CFE-DMHA could share administrative functions with host organization • Built-in agility to respond to quickly emerging requirements through access to a larger pool of overlapping expertise in both organizations
Unique weaknesses	• CFE-DMHA reputation may initially remain tied to its history • Need to develop and improve own processes, including assessment • May lack the flexibility to respond to rapidly evolving changes in requirements • May create friction and competition with regional centers • May create additional interagency friction on civ-mil coordination (USAID/OFDA)	• Challenge to maintain CFE-DMHA civ-mil DMHA coordination as a priority compared with traditional host-organization roles • Risk of CFE-DMHA's mission being influenced by host organization • Added bureaucratic layer within which CFE-DMHA must operate • Friction with regional centers and interagency may occur, but could be minimized through existing host-organization relationships
Order-of-magnitude estimate of required resources	• Estimated manpower: 68 • Estimated annual funding: $13M	• Estimated manpower: 59 • Estimated annual funding: $12M

Both COAs have strengths and weaknesses in common that derive from a broadening of CFE-DMHA's focus to a truly global orientation. A key strength of the global focus is that it provides the Secretary of Defense with a more direct means of applying CFE-DMHA's special authorities across CCMDs and regions. Consequently, CFE-DMHA would be able to address common needs across the CCMDs—and even address needs elsewhere in DoD—and span any seams between them to ensure global coverage of DMHA civ-mil coordination issues. Moreover, a global CFE-DMHA would be more responsive to CCMD requirements and more available to non-PACOM organizations. OSD could provide policy guidance and prioritize CFE-DMHA missions across the commands—for example, through a board chaired by a deputy assistant secretary of defense. Such a governance structure would resemble that of DoD regional centers, which are overseen and guided by a board of principal deputy assistant secretaries of defense, to which the centers semiannually report their plans and budgets. Finally, a decision to locate the core of the center in CONUS and provide CFE-DMHA experts in dispersed locations (e.g., liaisons at the CCMDs or at the Pentagon) could help expand relationships with domestic and foreign DMHA partners. It could also draw from a larger pool of expert personnel than is available in Hawaii.[67]

The common weaknesses of COAs 4 and 5 include a potential to dilute the effectiveness of CFE-DMHA in the Asia-Pacific region, where it has established important long-term relationships and shepherded key DMHA initiatives with ASEAN, OCHA, foreign-partner governments, and other regional partners. CFE-DMHA would need to act cautiously so as not to harm these relationships, squander expertise, or upset networks that have been carefully nurtured. Moreover, the transition to a global CFE-DMHA would need to avoid creating the perception that DoD has downgraded the role of DMHA in the Asia-Pacific despite the high priority accorded the region in U.S. national-security strategy. In all likelihood, the Asia-Pacific region would continue to be the highest-priority region even for a globally oriented CFE-DMHA.

A second common weakness is that CFE-DMHA would need to cultivate relationships and understand networks and cultures in other theaters from the ground up. However, a reconfigured CFE-DMHA could mitigate this challenge by hiring staff with well-established DMHA experience and expertise in these other theaters.

The two COAs also have unique strengths and weaknesses that help drive toward a recommended reconfiguration of a globally oriented CFE-DMHA. The unique strengths of the stand-alone organization relate to the ability of the director to independently engage OSD and the CCMDs on the development of the center's guidance and plans. This ability for the center director to directly engage CFE-DMHA's oversight entities would prevent the establishment of additional bureaucratic layers between the center and those overseeing, directing, and resourcing its missions and activities. The strengths of a center incorporated into an existing organization revolve around the ability to leverage the host organization's outlook, structures, expertise, networks, and processes. For example, the center's administrative functions would be absorbed by and shared with the host organization, and the center could adapt to existing processes that could enhance its own, such as assessment of performance. The center would adopt the host organization's global outlook and institutional culture to help it transition to a broader geographic focus and could benefit from the host organization's already-established under-

[67] Conversation with current or former CFE-DMHA staff, 2015; phone conversation with current or former EUCOM staff, 2015.

standing of and contributions to international networks in other regions. Moreover, assuming that the host organization pursues activities and retains expertise that overlap with those of CFE-DMHA, CFE-DMHA could draw on that expertise when rapidly evolving, short-term changes in requirements arise (such as a large disaster or other immediate needs, as directed by the Secretary of Defense). This would engender a highly agile organization. Perhaps most important, CFE-DMHA may be able to maintain or enhance its reputation in the Asia-Pacific while building it elsewhere through association with the host organization.

The unique weaknesses of the two COAs in large part mirror their strengths. While the stand-alone organization would minimize the bureaucratic layers between it and OSD, CFE-DMHA would need to broaden its own institutional processes and functions as it maintains its efforts in the Asia-Pacific while taking on new challenges (developing networks, building understanding of institutional cultures) in other regions. As an independent center, CFE-DMHA's reputation, which has been mixed (and, in some cases, unfavorable), could remain tied to its own history, at least initially. Moreover, a stand-alone organization likely would be less flexible in responding to quickly emerging changes in the type or scope of activities it must undertake and may be required to quickly seek outside contractors to fill these needs. Finally, while both COAs may create friction with DoD regional centers that conduct some DMHA-related activities (i.e., in education and research), as well as with such interagency partners as USAID and OFDA with the authority to lead U.S. international response efforts, a host organization with positive preexisting interactions with these other agencies may have an easier time smoothing out and nurturing more-cooperative relationships. On the other hand, a CFE-DMHA that is absorbed could compete with the host organization's own DMHA activities and may find the added bureaucratic layers problematic in its interactions with OSD and the CCMDs. The CFE-DMHA's missions could be influenced by the host organization's own vision and priorities, potentially leading to different interpretations of guidance provided to CFE-DMHA by OSD and the CCMDs.

We conclude that the unique strengths of COA 5 outweigh its weaknesses and would put CFE-DMHA in a better overall position than COA 4. These strengths, in combination with efforts to improve the health of the organization (as described in Chapter Three), would enable CFE-DMHA to address the challenges of a global mandate and provide the institution with attributes it has lacked for much of its history. The ability of an absorbed CFE-DMHA to leverage a host organization's networks, outlook, and administrative functions as it moves to a global orientation is a strong advantage over an independent CFE-DMHA that must create and sustain these itself.

Several organizations could be strong candidates to serve as host for CFE-DMHA under COA 5, and each has advantages and disadvantages. CCMR appears to have important advantages in its focus on civ-mil affairs, a slate of DMHA-related efforts, and global networks. PDC is established globally, though its main focus (as indicated by its name) is in the Pacific. However, its orientation is decidedly technological, with its main efforts on its disaster applications and software. Another candidate is the Center for Complex Operations at the National Defense University in Washington, D.C., which has strong education and training and information clearinghouse roles; however, its focus on a wide range of operations may dilute the impact of CFE-DMHA's efforts in DMHA. A closer examination of the process for merging these organizations with CFE-DMHA, and of the effects of such a merger on relationships with outside organizations, is obviously required but was beyond the scope of the present study.

As mentioned previously, it was also beyond the scope of this study to conduct a cost analysis of CFE-DMHA COAs. We can, however, provide an order-of-magnitude estimate of the resources that a globally oriented CFE-DMHA might require to execute key activities for recommended Title 10 missions. As described in Chapter Three, the current CFE-DMHA director has undertaken an initiative to rationalize the activities and missions that CFE-DMHA pursues with the resources that PACOM and other funding sources provide. This initiative provides the case for conducting "required activities" in education and training, regional engagement, and information sharing (which includes lessons learned) at an FY 2016 core funding level of $4.8 million, with current manning.[68] This narrowing of activities for CFE-DMHA in the Asia-Pacific agrees with the mission and activity recommendations in this report and provides a lower bound to the resources required to execute priority missions globally. At the other end of the spectrum is a 2009 manpower review that analyzed the unconstrained resource requirements of a CFE-DMHA that conducts all of its Title 10 missions globally. That study concluded that CFE-DMHA needed 45 DoD employees and 24 contractors, for a total of 69, at an estimated cost of $15.5 million per year.[69] This provides an upper bound to our estimate, since we recommend that CFE-DMHA focus globally on a subset of its Title 10 missions and associated activities but with some expansion in scope. Generally, then, the recommendation to move to a globally oriented organization is contingent on the availability of higher funding levels for CFE-DMHA.

The stand-alone center would require an estimated 68 personnel and $13 million in core funding, which includes O&M and civilian pay. A center that is incorporated into an existing globally oriented organization would require an estimated 59 personnel and about $12 million in core funding. The primary difference in required resources between the two COAs is based on administrative functions and institutional capital.[70] The actual difference in cost to the USG is likely to be less than $1 million and nine employees; even if there are some overall savings from consolidation of "back office" functions, it can be assumed that a host organization would need to allocate some additional staff and funds to provide administrative support to CFE-DMHA. As a result, the overall difference in resources required for COAs 4 and 5 would not be very significant, but COA 5 would appear to be somewhat less expensive than COA 4—an additional benefit to pursuing alignment with an existing organization. Determining the real cost of either of these COAs would require an in-depth analysis of the actual organizational and operational concepts that would be applied to a reconfigured CFE-DMHA. This was beyond the scope of the present study but is essential to inform decisions about CFE-DMHA's future. It is possible that resource requirements will be higher than we estimate, given expanded activities in education and training, engagement, and research and information sharing, despite the reduction in missions.

---

[68] This includes civilian pay, with the hiring of three additional DoD civilians offset by three departing contractors, for a DoD manpower total of nine, plus 19 full-time-equivalent contractors. CFE-DMHA, 2015d. However, according to one interlocutor, this would still not be an adequate number of DoD civilians to ensure the health of CFE-DMHA under current circumstances. Conversation with current or former CFE-DMHA official, 2015.

[69] CFE-DMHA, 2015d.

[70] This analysis reflects assumptions from the 2009 manpower review, including specific positions and the mix of DoD employees and contractors—and average personnel and O&M costs of CFE-DMHA today. The RAND analysis alters some of the personnel numbers and positions based on the mission and geographic focus recommendations in this report. But this is by no means a substitute for an in-depth cost analysis that revisits the assumptions of both the 2009 review and the RAND analysis.

In sum, based on our understanding of CFE-DMHA's history and activities, our findings about mission and geographic focus, as well as the strengths and weaknesses of alternative courses of action, we conclude that OSD should direct that CFE-DMHA be merged with an existing, globally oriented DoD organization with overlapping roles. This recommendation is based on the strengths of this COA in terms of the ability of a reconfigured CFE-DMHA to leverage existing institutional outlook, reputation, functions, and relationships. And while required resources would be higher than those of CFE-DMHA in its current form, the option of an absorbed CFE-DMHA with a global orientation would be somewhat cheaper than the alternative option of an independent organization. With appropriate resources, this would allow a newly configured, globally focused CFE-DMHA to more quickly build networks and relationships in other theaters; to rebuild its brand as a reliable, effective partner in DMHA efforts; and to share functions with the host organization to help minimize costs.

CHAPTER FIVE

Conclusion

CFE-DMHA is at a critical time in its existence. It has been struggling for years to fulfill a broad set of disaster-management missions and activities set by Congress and DoD, which one discussant described as "a mile wide."[1] The perennial mismatch between the requirements and the funding CFE-DMHA receives makes it necessary for the center to focus on those areas that have the greatest return on investment.[2] While the current CFE-DMHA director is seeking to implement such a strategy, and his efforts could put the center in a better position over time to pursue core disaster management activities, this is not likely to solve all of the issues that the center has been experiencing for years. CFE-DMHA will need a number of improvements—in addition to resources that match its mission—that will allow it to operate as a distinct center and become a healthier organization. Such improvements include implementing guidance that provides more oversight over the activities and missions the center pursues in the near term; consistent, adequate core funding over the long term that is not subject to changing priorities in a single theater; a more favorable manpower mix that raises the ratio of USG and contract employees; widely recognized DMHA experts on staff, with development and retention of this expertise from both military and civilian sectors; and a director hired competitively with full coordination among the key stakeholders.

In sum, CFE-DMHA should be resourced adequately and reconfigured to pursue Title 10 missions globally where there are important gaps, where CFE-DMHA would have a competitive advantage, and where CFE-DMHA's role is unique. CFE-DMHA cannot accomplish this in its current form or with existing levels of resources. There is a need for a continued high level of CFE-DMHA activity in the Asia-Pacific, but there are also needs across DoD and in other regions that could be filled by a global DMHA entity. This would require an organization with a truly global outlook. Our review of alternative courses of action has led us to conclude that OSD should pursue an option of aligning CFE-DMHA with an existing globally oriented DoD institution with overlapping activities. This option would enable CFE-DMHA to adopt and share the host organization's culture and outlook, administrative functions, processes, and established networks and could leverage the host's reputation to enhance its own. If CFE-DMHA is to fulfill these needs, it will need to be recast and provided the necessary guidance, resources, and organizational structure.

A globally oriented CFE-DMHA would be reconfigured to incorporate the improvements mentioned above and to expand its education and training, strengthen its research and repository functions, and broaden its regional engagement capacity. This CFE-DMHA would

---

[1]   Phone conversation with current or former CFE-DMHA staff, 2014.

[2]   Conversation with current or former CFE-DMHA staff, 2015.

have a central core of DMHA staff (who may be physically located or virtually aligned with the host organization) and experts assigned to CCMDs as needed. Most of this staff could reside in the PACOM AOR in a "Pacific first" approach, with reachback to the core. There could also be a liaison element in the Washington, D.C., area to interact frequently with OSD and DSCA on the programs and initiatives CFE-DMHA is undertaking and to serve as the "eyes and ears" of CFE-DMHA and host-organization directors in Washington. CFE-DMHA's success would be conditioned on adequate resources that match its roles and missions and the direction that DoD decisionmakers desire for it in the future. Regardless of the way ahead, centralizing financial control in Washington may be a way to help ensure CFE-DMHA's future stability and effectiveness.

This report sought to provide insight on the history and activities of CFE-DMHA, shed light on the continuing need for a DMHA organization in DoD, and explore options for its future pursuits. As noted, further analysis in a number of areas is warranted, which was beyond the scope of the research in this report. Detailed assessment of global DMHA requirements, candidate organizations for CFE-DMHA alignment, transition processes, staffing needs, and costs would support DoD decisions on how CFE-DMHA should be reconfigured. Notwithstanding this additional analysis, our research leads us to conclusions and recommendations aimed at better positioning CFE-DMHA to meet ongoing needs to enhance civ-mil coordination in DoD for DMHA.

Language of Title 10, Section 182

CFE-DMHA's charter stems from a congressional authority that was introduced by public law into Title 10 in November 1997. It resides within Title 10 (Armed Forces) under Subtitle A (General Military Law), Part I (Organization and General Military Powers), Chapter 7 (Boards, Councils, and Committees).

Section 182: Center for Excellence in Disaster Management and Humanitarian Assistance

(a) Establishment.—The Secretary of Defense may operate a Center for Excellence in Disaster Management and Humanitarian Assistance (in this section referred to as the "Center").
(b) Missions.—
   (1) The Center shall be used to provide and facilitate education, training, and research in civil-military operations, particularly operations that require international disaster management and humanitarian assistance and operations that require coordination between the Department of Defense and other agencies.
   (2) The Center shall be used to make available high-quality disaster management and humanitarian assistance in response to disasters.
   (3) The Center shall be used to provide and facilitate education, training, interagency coordination, and research on the following additional matters:
      (A) Management of the consequences of nuclear, biological, and chemical events.
      (B) Management of the consequences of terrorism.
      (C) Appropriate roles for the reserve components in the management of such consequences and in disaster management and humanitarian assistance in response to natural disasters.
      (D) Meeting requirements for information in connection with regional and global disasters, including the use of advanced communications technology as a virtual library.
      (E) Tropical medicine, particularly in relation to the medical readiness requirements of the Department of Defense.
   (4) The Center shall develop a repository of disaster risk indicators for the Asia-Pacific region.
   (5) The Center shall perform such other missions as the Secretary of Defense may specify.
(c) Joint Operation With Educational Institution Authorized.—The Secretary of Defense may enter into an agreement with appropriate officials of an institution of higher education to provide for joint operation of the Center. Any such agreement shall provide for the institution to

furnish necessary administrative services for the Center, including administration and allocation of funds.

(d) Acceptance of Donations.—

(1) Except as provided in paragraph (2), the Secretary of Defense may accept, on behalf of the Center, donations to be used to defray the costs of the Center or to enhance the operation of the Center. Such donations may be accepted from any agency of the Federal Government, any State or local government, any foreign government, any foundation or other charitable organization (including any that is organized or operates under the laws of a foreign country), or any other private source in the United States or a foreign country.

(2) The Secretary may not accept a donation under paragraph (1) if the acceptance of the donation would compromise or appear to compromise—

(A) the ability of the Department of Defense, any employee of the Department, or members of the armed forces, to carry out any responsibility or duty of the Department in a fair and objective manner; or

(B) the integrity of any program of the Department of Defense or of any person involved in such a program.

(3) The Secretary shall prescribe written guidance setting forth the criteria to be used in determining whether or not the acceptance of a foreign donation would have a result described in paragraph (2).

(4) Funds accepted by the Secretary under paragraph (1) as a donation on behalf of the Center shall be credited to appropriations available to the Department of Defense for the Center. Funds so credited shall be merged with the appropriations to which credited and shall be available for the Center for the same purposes and the same period as the appropriations with which merged.[1]

Payments for Education and Training of Personnel of Foreign Countries

The authority was further amended in 2002 by public law:

> During the current fiscal year and hereafter, under regulations prescribed by the Secretary of Defense, the Center of Excellence for Disaster Management and Humanitarian Assistance [this should probably be Center *for* Excellence in Disaster Management and Humanitarian Assistance] may also pay, or authorize payment for, the expenses of providing or facilitating education and training for appropriate military and civilian personnel of foreign countries in disaster management, peace operations, and humanitarian assistance.[2]

Similar provisions were contained in prior appropriation acts.[3]

---

[1]   Public Law 105–85, 1997.

[2]   Public Law 107–248, 2002.

[3]   Public Law 107-117, Department of Defense and Emergency Supplemental Appropriations for Recovery from and Response to Terrorist Attacks on the U.S. Act, 2002, Sec. 8109, January 10, 2002; Public Law 106-79, Appropriations for the Department of Defense for Fiscal Year 2003, Sec. 8093, October 25, 1999.

Improving CFE-DMHA's Ability to Self-Assess

CFE-DMHA is not the only security-cooperation organization to find self-assessment challenging. Most organizations do not devote the resources or expertise needed to conduct thorough program evaluations or assessments of organizational effectiveness. Even when such resources might be available, the challenges to effective program evaluation are numerous, especially for organizations with abstract and broad missions that may require executing tasks for several years before positive impact can be realized. Further complicating valid assessments of program effectiveness are external factors (e.g., political processes, other HADR programs) that could directly or indirectly affect the success or failure of a program. Although external factors are often outside the control of a specific program, steps should be taken to identify such factors and the extent to which they can account for a program's success or failure.

Other members of organizations working on HADR issues interviewed for this study confirmed these difficulties. One noted asking participants, at the end of workshops, how valuable they thought the engagement was.[1] Evaluating how much participants enjoyed a program is relatively easy; evaluating how much they learned from it is the harder part. One organization interviewed considered implementing a pre- and post-test to compare the participants' knowledge of an issue before and after the engagement, but the method was deemed as a potential source of embarrassment for participants who may feel uneasy at being tested on their knowledge. In other words, assessment would have hampered the relation-building value of the activity.[2] Even in such cases, however, the host nation or country teams can help to identify alternative methods. For example, individual assessment viewed as direct feedback at the individual level may not be widely accepted in some cultures, but one alternative could be to place training participants into small groups to work as a team to take assessments. When cultural barriers are anticipated, steps should be taken to openly discuss options, especially since research finds that many cultural barriers have been overstated.[3]

Another important measure of performance, albeit equally difficult to operationalize, is how much of the knowledge imparted during courses or workshops "sticks" with participants. Participants could be contacted six months, one year, or two years later to fill a similar questionnaire as the exit one. Yet, in practice, very few organizations follow up with their

---

[1] Phone conversation with current or former HADR organization staff, 2015. This is done by asking the participants to fill out an evaluation form.

[2] Phone conversation with current or former HADR organization staff, 2015.

[3] Ann Marie Ryan and Nancy T. Tippins, "Global Applications of Assessment," in John C. Scott and Douglas H. Reynolds, eds., *Handbook of Workplace Assessment: Evidence-Based Practices for Selecting and Developing Organizational Talent*, San Francisco: Jossey-Bass, 2010.

alumni because of lack of dedicated resources. In many cases, project funds last for only a year, making it impossible to set aside a fraction of it for follow-up.[4] Regional centers are an exception, because they have made alumni outreach one of their priorities.[5] This, however, requires a sizable amount of resources (APCSS, for instance, has two staff members in charge of relations with alumni[6]) that smaller organizations, such as CFE-DMHA, cannot spare. It is also a hazardous process. One organization interviewed for this study noted that it used to send follow-up surveys to its alumni between six months and two years after the activity but did not get a good return rate at all.[7]

Beyond the skills acquired, other benefits of engagement, such as better relations and increased access, are even harder to measure. One discussant who manages a DMHA-related program noted that learning goes in both directions: Events with partner nations are also a conduit for the United States to better understand them, and possibly, over time and through broader diplomatic means, affect policy change in these countries.[8] Overall, however, most activities trigger very little change in the short term.[9] This does not mean that these events, in the broader picture, do not have value—just that this value is excessively hard to measure.

Yet, despite the challenges to program evaluation, many organizations, including DoD organizations and NGOs, are experiencing increased pressure to measure program effectiveness because funding sources, lawmakers, and the public have called for increased accountability. For example, a Government Accountability Office report in 2012 focused on humanitarian and development assistance across civilian agencies (Department of State and the USAID) and DoD found: "From fiscal years, 2005 through 2009, DoD had not completed 90 percent of the required 1-year post-project evaluations for its OHDACA projects, and about half of the required 30-day evaluations for those projects, and thus lacks information to determine projects' effects."[10] Without adequate evaluation information on program impacts, Congress has limited information for determining appropriateness when allocating funds among the various programs in future budgets. Because of the challenges of program evaluation, several frameworks and guides have been developed to support organizations' effort to evaluate the effectiveness of their programs.

The metrics chosen to assess one's performance are critical because they reflect the ultimate goal for which the organization was set up. In the case of CFE-DMHA, two discussants independently cited impact on victims of disasters as the first and foremost metric for what CFE-DMHA does.[11] The operating principle for the center should then be to determine whether there is a connection between improvements in victims on the ground post-disaster

---

[4]   Phone conversation with current or former HADR organization staff, 2015.

[5]   Hanauer et al., 2014, p. 60.

[6]   APCSS is also the only regional center to have put in place measurable standards for its programs and a systematic data collection plan (Hanauer et al., 2014, p. 107).

[7]   Conversation with current or former HADR organization staff, 2015.

[8]   Phone conversation with current or former HADR organization staff, 2015.

[9]   Phone conversation with current or former HADR organization staff, 2015.

[10]   U.S. Government Accountability Office, *Humanitarian and Development Assistance: Project Evaluations and Better Information Sharing Needed to Manage the Military's Efforts*, GAO-12-359, February 8, 2012.

[11]   Conversation with current or former CFE-DMHA staff, 2015; conversation with current or former CFE-DMHA staff, 2015.

and the work done by CFE-DMHA.[12] As of 2015, CFE-DMHA was reportedly looking into ways to improve its assessment process. One idea was to build an assessment checklist that someone from PACOM—with expertise in the focus area of the program being assessed (e.g., health, disaster management)—would implement.[13]

Recognizing the challenges of program evaluation, several frameworks and guides have been developed to support organizations' efforts to evaluate the effectiveness of their programs. One of the most widely used frameworks for guiding program evaluations is the logic model, which has been used by program evaluators for more than 30 years.[14] Logic models are also used frequently by U.S. and international government agencies, as well as HADR organizations.

Based on program theory, a logic model establishes a systematic plan for how a program is supposed to work.[15] That is, the plan or model defines the inputs, activities, and outputs required to address a specific problem (see Figure B.1). One example of a long-term outcome might be to ensure regional stability in the event of a natural disaster. To accomplish this mission, a program might provide education and training workshops (outputs) to increase participants' knowledge of laws and regulations of a specific country prone to typhoons (short-term outcomes). This increased knowledge should guide participants' behaviors when responding to an emergency in this country, which may help to avoid potential conflict and delays in providing aid (intermediate outcomes). Ultimately, the education and training provided results in a more resilient and stable country over the long term by increasing the ability to rapidly respond to the specific country's needs following a disaster. The specific elements of a logic model and examples are provided in Table B.1.

An effective logic model should specify the why and how for major program activities within an organization. That is, why are we doing this specific activity and how will it help to achieve a specific outcome. A clearly defined logic model not only helps to provide a theory for an organization but also supports the development of metrics for program evaluation by targeting specific short-term, intermediate, and long-term outcomes that should be affected by a specific program activity. Understandably, most organizations have more data available to track outputs than outcomes. It is relatively easy to measure and count outputs or deliv-

Figure B.1
Logic Model Flowchart

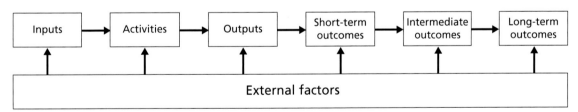

---

[12] Conversation with current or former CFE-DMHA staff, 2015.

[13] Conversation with current or former CFE-DMHA staff, 2015.

[14] J. A. McLaughlin and G. B. Jordan, "Logic Models: A Tool for Telling Your Programs Performance Story," *Evaluation and Program Planning*, Vol. 22, No. 1, 1999.

[15] Leonard Bickman, "The Functions of Program Theory," *New Directions for Program Evaluation*, Vol. 1987, No. 33, 1987.

Table B.1
Elements of a Logic Model

Element	Description	Example
Inputs	• Resources required to engage in organizational activities	• Financial resources • Core funding • Variable funding • Time • Personnel • Permanent staff • Contractors • Partnerships • Building facilities and equipment
Activities	• Processes and actions taken by the organization to achieve desired outputs	• Conducting applied research • Providing training workshops • Providing subject-matter expertise at seminars
Outputs	• Products and services provided by the organization • Deliverables	• Lessons-learned documents • Humanitarian reference documents • HART course
Short-term outcomes	• Desired changes immediately affected by outputs • May include changes in knowledge, skills, attitudes, and awareness targeted by outputs	• Increased knowledge of mechanisms to coordinate response to a disaster • Increased knowledge of risks faced by a specific country
Intermediate outcomes	• Desired changes in behaviors, which should result from changes in knowledge, skills, etc. • May include changes in planning, budgeting, coordinating activities	• Increased number of disaster exercises conducted by a specific country • Increased demand for a specific training course • Development of infrastructure to respond more efficiently to a disaster
Long-term outcomes	• Defined by the overarching purpose and mission of the program • May include desired changes in political, societal, and economic conditions within specific regions of the world	• Increased stability and security in a specific region of the world • Increased resilience within a specific region of the world
External factors	• Any factor outside the program or organization that influences program activities, outputs, or outcomes • May include different types of influencers—some may contribute positively to program goals and others may interfere or detract from program goals	• Host-nation political stability • Host-nation perceptions of U.S. military forces and DoD • U.S. political interests

erables (e.g., how many reports were produced). Much more difficult is the task to evaluate the impact that those reports have on an intended audience. Nonetheless, a logic model can help direct organizations' program-evaluation efforts by clarifying the ways in which specific outputs should affect short-term, intermediate, and long-term outcomes. For example, if the purpose of a report is to increase awareness and shape attitudes, then specific measures can be developed to evaluate the extent to which readers' attitudes changed.

Program-evaluation specialists should be consulted when planning or developing measures to track outcomes to reduce or eliminate alternative explanations for an outcome. Although external factors (e.g., host-country laws) can affect several parts of the logic model, they will most likely affect interpretations of causality for long-term outcomes. That is, external factors are more likely to occur as the time between a program's outputs and desired outcomes increases. Therefore, a program evaluation specialist can recommend which external factors should also be monitored and may also provide guidance on an appropriate research methodology for evaluating a program's impact.

Abbreviations

AFRICOM	U.S. Africa Command
AOR	area of responsibility
APCSS	Asia-Pacific Center for Security Studies
APRI	Asia-Pacific Regional Initiative
ASD/SOLIC	Assistant Secretary of Defense for Special Operations and Low-Intensity Conflict
ASEAN	Association of Southeast Asian Nations
BCA	business case analysis
CBRN	chemical, biological, radiological, and nuclear
CCMD	combatant command
CCMR	Center for Civil-Military Relations
CDC	Centers for Disease Control and Prevention
CDHAM	Center for Disaster and Humanitarian Assistance Medicine
CENTCOM	U.S. Central Command
CFE	Center for Excellence
CFE-DMHA	Center for Excellence in Disaster Management and Humanitarian Assistance
CHART	Combined Humanitarian Assistance Response Training
CHIP	CFE-DMHA Humanitarian Information Paper
civ-mil	civil-military
CMEP	Civil-Military Emergency Preparedness Program
COA	course of action
COE-DMHA	Center of Excellence in Disaster Management and Humanitarian Assistance
DMHA	disaster management and humanitarian assistance

DoD	Department of Defense
DRU	Direct Reporting Unit
DSCA	Defense Security Cooperation Agency
DTRA	Defense Threat Response Agency
EUCOM	U.S. European Command
FEMA	Federal Emergency Management Agency
FY	fiscal year
HADR	humanitarian assistance and disaster relief
HART	Humanitarian Assistance Response Training
HDM	HADR, Disaster Relief and Mine Action
H.E.L.P.	Health Emergencies in Large Populations
IG	inspector general
JHOC	Joint Humanitarian Operations Course
MOU	memorandum of understanding
NGO	nongovernmental organization
NORTHCOM	U.S. Northern Command
O&M	operations and maintenance
OCHA	United Nations Office for the Coordination of Humanitarian Affairs
OFDA	Office of Foreign Disaster Assistance
OHDACA	Overseas Humanitarian, Disaster, and Civic Aid
OSD	Office of the Secretary of Defense
PACOM	U.S. Pacific Command
PDC	Pacific Disaster Center
PDMIN	Pacific Disaster Management Information Network
SME	subject-matter expert
SOUTHCOM	U.S. Southern Command
TRACS	The Resiliency Analysis and Coordination System
UN-CMCoord	United Nation Civil-Military Coordination
USAID	U.S. Agency for International Development
U.S.C.	United States Code

USD/P	Under Secretary of Defense for Policy
USG	U.S. government
USPACOM	U.S. Pacific Command
USPACOMINST	U.S. Pacific Command instruction
WIF	Warsaw Initiative Fund

References

ASD/SOLIC—*See* U.S. Assistant Secretary of Defense for Special Operations/Low-Intensity Conflict.

Bickman, Leonard, "The Functions of Program Theory," *New Directions for Program Evaluation*, Vol. 1987, No. 33, 1987, pp. 5–18.

Blair, Dennis C., "Statement of Admiral Dennis C. Blair, U.S. Navy Commander in Chief, U.S. Pacific Command, Before a subcommittee of the Committee on Appropriations," U.S. Senate, 107th Congress, Special Hearing, April 3, 2002. As of July 5, 2015:
http://www.gpo.gov/fdsys/pkg/CHRG-107shrg80485/html/CHRG-107shrg80485.htm

Brewer, G. A., and S. C. Selden, "Why Elephants Gallop: Assessing and Predicting Organizational Performance in Federal Agencies," *Journal of Public Administration Research and Theory*, Vol. 10, No. 4, 2000, pp. 685–712.

Center for Excellence in Disaster Management and Humanitarian Assistance, *Center for Excellence in Disaster Management and Humanitarian Assistance (CFE-DMHA) FY12 Events*, internal document, Ford Island, Hawaii, undated-a.

———, *CFE Funding—Historic Graph*, internal briefing, Ford Island, Hawaii, undated-b.

———, "CFE Manpower-Task Comparison," briefing slides, internal document, Ford Island, Hawaii, undated-c.

———, *FY 2011 Theater Campaign Plan Event Summary, Center for Excellence in Disaster Management and Humanitarian Assistance*, internal document, Ford Island, Hawaii, undated-d.

———, *H.E.L.P. Course Critique Summary Spreadsheet*, internal document, Ford Island, Hawaii, undated-e.

———, *Organizational History, 1 January–31 December 2012*, Ford Island, Hawaii, 2013.

———, *Strategy FY2014–2018*, Ford Island, Hawaii, January 2014a.

———, *Strategy to Task Analysis*, briefing, Ford Island, Hawaii, August 22, 2014b.

———, *CFE-DMHA Web Presence, Measures of Performance*, briefing, internal document, Ford Island, Hawaii, January 2015a.

———, *Rohingya Crisis*, Ford Island, Hawaii, Humanitarian Information Paper No. 1, Ford Island, Hawaii, May 22, 2015b. As of October 6, 2015:
http://reliefweb.int/sites/reliefweb.int/files/resources/150522_U_CHIP_RohingyaCrisis.pdf

———, *Subject: Disaster Management Country Assessment Program*, information paper, internal document, Ford Island, Hawaii, June 18, 2015c.

———, untitled briefing slides, internal document, Ford Island, Hawaii, July 14, 2015d.

———, *Information Paper; Subject: Center for Excellence in Disaster Management (CFE-DM) Communication Platforms and Product Metrics from January to July 2015*, Ford Island, Hawaii, August 10, 2015e.

———, *Meeting Disaster Management Challenges with Excellence: Program Plan FY16–20*, Ford Island, Hawaii, October 1, 2015f.

———, *Command History: January 1–December 31, 2014*, Ford Island, Hawaii, 2015g.

Center of Excellence in Disaster Management and Humanitarian Assistance, *1998 Annual Report*, Honolulu, undated-a.

———, *1999 Annual Report*, Honolulu, undated-b.

———, *COE DMHA Events Fiscal Year 2010*, internal document, Honolulu, undated-c.

———, *Fiscal Year 2001 Annual Report*, Honolulu, undated-d.

———, *Mid-Year Activity Report*, Honolulu, 2002.

———, *2010 Command History, Annex J to U.S. Pacific Command History, 1 January–31 December 2010*, Honolulu, 2010.

———, *Business Case Analysis*, briefing, internal document, Honolulu, May 2012a.

———, "COE-DMHA: Manpower Review Briefing," briefing slides, internal document, Honolulu, November 21, 2012b.

———, *Business Case Analysis*, manpower review briefing, Honolulu, November 2012c.

———, *Deliverables*, briefing, Honolulu, 2012d.

"CFE-DM Initiatives," Center for Excellence in Disaster Management and Humanitarian Assistance, undated. As of March 28, 2016:
https://www.cfe-dmha.org/About-CFE-DM/CFE-DM-Initiatives

CFE-DMHA—*See* Center for Excellence in Disaster Management and Humanitarian Assistance.

"Chemical Biological Incident Response Force," U.S. Marine Corps, undated. As of May 25, 2015:
http://www.cbirf.marines.mil/UnitHome.aspx

COE-DMHA—*See* Center of Excellence in Disaster Management and Humanitarian Assistance.

Combs, J., Yongmei Liu, Angela Hall, and David Ketchen, "How Much Do High-Performance Work Practices Matter? A Meta-Analysis of Their Effects on Organizational Performance," *Personnel Psychology*, Vol. 59, No. 3, 2006, pp. 501–528.

Craig, William, Matthew Fisher, Suzanne Garcia-Miller, Clay Kaylor, and John Porter, *Generalized Criteria and Evaluation Method for Center of Excellence: A Preliminary Report*, Pittsburgh, Pa.: Carnegie Mellon University, December 2009.

Defense Security Cooperation Agency, "Humanitarian Assistance and Mine Action Programs," in *Security Assistance Management Manual*, last revised October 1, 2015. As of October 7, 2015:
http://www.samm.dsca.mil/chapter/chapter-12#C12.4

"Disaster Management Agencies Sign Bilateral Agreements," Pacific Disaster Center, July 25, 2014. As of July 29, 2015:
http://www.pdc.org/news-n-media/pdc-updates/Disaster_Management_Agencies_Sign_Bilateral_Agreements/

"Disaster Management Reference Handbooks," Center for Excellence in Disaster Management and Humanitarian Assistance, undated. As of July 29, 2015:
https://www.cfe-dmha.org/DMHA-Resources/Disaster-Management-Reference-Handbooks.

"DMHA Partners," Center for Excellence in Disaster Management and Humanitarian Assistance, undated. As of July 29, 2015:
https://www.cfe-dmha.org/Partnerships

DoD—*See* U.S. Department of Defense.

DSCA—*See* Defense Security Cooperation Agency.

Federal Register, Vol. 76, No. 176, Washington, D.C.: U.S. Government Printing Office, September 12, 2011.

Hanauer, Larry, Stuart E. Johnson, Christopher J. Springer, Chaoling Feng, Michael J. McNerney, Stephanie Pezard, and Shira Efron, *Evaluating the Impact of the Department of Defense Regional Centers for Security Studies*, Santa Monica, Calif.: RAND Corporation, RR-388-OSD, 2014. As of October 5, 2015:
http://www.rand.org/pubs/research_reports/RR388

"Health Emergencies in Large Populations (H.E.L.P.) Course," Center for Excellence in Disaster Management and Humanitarian Assistance, undated. As of July 31, 2015:
https://www.cfe-dmha.org/Training/Health-Emergencies-in-Large-Populations-HELP-Course

"Humanitarian Assistance Response Training (HART) Course," Center for Excellence in Disaster Management and Humanitarian Assistance, undated. As of July 31, 2015:
https://www.cfe-dmha.org/Training/Humanitarian-Assistance-Response-Training-HART-Course

"Information Papers: Institutional Training Under Centers of Excellence," U.S. Army, undated. As of October 10, 2015:
http://www.army.mil/aps/08/information_papers/transform/Institutional_Training.html

Jiang, K., D. P. Lepak, J. Hu, and J. C. Baer, "How Does Human Resource Management Influence Organizational Outcomes? A Meta-Analytic Investigation of Mediating Mechanisms," *Academy of Management Journal*, Vol. 55, No. 6, 2012, pp. 1264–1294.

"Lessons Learned," Center for Excellence in Disaster Management and Humanitarian Assistance, undated. As of October 10, 2015:
https://www.cfe-dmha.org/Resources/Lessons-Learned

"Liaison," Center for Excellence in Disaster Management and Humanitarian Assistance, undated. As of July 29, 2015:
https://www.cfe-dmha.org/Liaison/Liaison-Archives

McLaughlin, J. A., and G. B. Jordan, "Logic Models: A Tool for Telling Your Program's Performance Story," *Evaluation and Program Planning*, Vol. 22, No. 1, 1999, pp. 65–72.

Mead, Phil, *COE-DMHA Strategy and Organization Decision Brief*, Ford Island, Hawaii: Center for Excellence in Disaster Management and Humanitarian Assistance, September 18, 2011.

Moroney, Jennifer D., Stephanie Pezard, Laurel E. Miller, Jeffrey Engstrom, and Abby Doll, *Lessons from Department of Defense Disaster Relief Efforts in the Asia-Pacific Region*, Santa Monica, Calif.: RAND Corporation, RR-146-OSD, 2013. As of October 6, 2015:
http://www.rand.org/pubs/research_reports/RR146

Muldrow, T. W., Timothy Buckley, and B. W. Schay, "Creating High-Performance Organizations in the Public Sector," *Human Resource Management*, Vol. 41, No. 3, 2002, pp. 341–354.

National Defense Authorization Act Fiscal Year 1994, Senate Conference Report for House Resolution 2401, January 1993.

Obama, Barack, *National Security Strategy*, Washington, D.C.: White House, February 2015.

OCHA—*See* United Nations Office for the Coordination of Humanitarian Affairs.

PACOM—*See* U.S. Pacific Command.

Prawdzik, Chris, "Preparing Partners for Emergencies," Defense Media Network, March 14, 2011. As of July 23, 2015:
http://www.defensemedianetwork.com/stories/preparing-partners-for-emergencies

Public Law 105-85, Title III, Sec. 382 Center for Excellence in Disaster Management and Humanitarian Assistance, November 18, 1997.

Public Law 106-79, Appropriations for the Department of Defense for Fiscal Year 2003, Sec. 8093, October 25, 1999.

Public Law 106-259, Department of Defense Appropriations Act, 2001, Sec. 8109, August 9, 2000.

Public Law 107-117, Department of Defense and Emergency Supplemental Appropriations for Recovery from and Response to Terrorist Attacks on the U.S. Act, 2002, Sec. 8109, January 10, 2002.

Public Law 107-248, Appropriations for the Department of Defense for Fiscal Year 2003, Sec. 8093, October 23, 2002.

Rainey, Hal G., and Paula Steinbauer, "Galloping Elephants: Developing Elements of a Theory of Effective Government Organizations," *Journal of Public Administration Research and Theory*, Vol. 1, September 1999, pp. 1–32.

Riebeek, Holli, "The Rising Cost of Natural Hazards," NASA Earth Observatory, March 28, 2005. As of June 24, 2015:
http://earthobservatory.nasa.gov/Features/RisingCost/printall.php

Ryan, Ann Marie, and Nancy T. Tippins, "Global Applications of Assessment," in John C. Scott and Douglas H. Reynolds, eds., *Handbook of Workplace Assessment: Evidence-Based Practices for Selecting and Developing Organizational Talent*, San Francisco: Jossey-Bass, 2010, pp. 577–606.

"Strategy to Task Analysis," Center for Excellence in Disaster Management and Humanitarian Assistance, undated. As of July 29, 2015:
https://www.cfe-dmha.org/About-CFE-DMHA/Hierarchy-of-Strategies-Plans-and-Doctrine-for-DMHA

Tang, Alisa, "After Decades of Disasters, U.N. Shifts Its Asia Operations," Reuters, June 29, 2015.

"Training Courses," Center for Excellence in Disaster Management and Humanitarian Assistance, undated. As of July 31, 2015:
https://www.cfe-dmha.org/Training/Other-DMHA-Training

United Nations Office for the Coordination of Humanitarian Affairs "UN-CMCoord Training and Partnership Programme, Calendar of Events, 2015," 2015. As of October 9, 2015:
https://docs.unocha.org/sites/dms/Documents/150721%20Calendar%20of%20Activities%202015.pdf

United States Code, Title 10, Sec. 182, Center for Excellence in Disaster Management and Humanitarian Assistance, January 3, 2012.

United States Code, Title 31, Money and Finance, Sec. 501, Office of Management and Budget, 2011.

U.S. Army Training and Doctrine Command Regulation 10-5-5, *United States Army Combined Arms Support Command and Sustainment Center of Excellence*, Fort Monroe, Va.: Department of the Army, Headquarters, September 10, 2010.

U.S. Assistant Secretary of Defense, Special Operations/Low-Intensity Conflict, "Memorandum for Commander, U.S. Pacific Command; Subject: Policy Guidance for Center for Excellence in Disaster Management and Humanitarian Assistance (CFE)," October 18, 2013.

U.S. Department of Defense, *Quadrennial Defense Review Report*, Washington, D.C., February 2010.

———, *The National Military Strategy of the United States of America 2015*, Washington, D.C., June 2015.

U.S. Deputy Secretary of Defense, "Memorandum for Director, Center of Excellence in Disaster Management and Humanitarian Assistance; Subject: Authority to Accept Donations," May 10, 2004.

U.S. Europe Command and the Center for Excellence in Disaster Management and Humanitarian Assistance, memorandum of agreement, Revision 1, October 6, 2011.

U.S. Government Accountability Office, *Humanitarian and Development Assistance: Project Evaluations and Better Information Sharing Needed to Manage the Military's Efforts*, Washington, D.C., GAO-12-359, February 8, 2012.

U.S. Office of Personnel Management, *Delegated Examining Operations Handbook: A Guide for Federal Agency Examining Offices*, Washington, D.C., May 2007. As of July 31, 2015:
https://www.opm.gov/policy-data-oversight/hiring-authorities/competitive-hiring/deo_handbook.pdf

U.S. Pacific Command, "Decision Memo; Subject: (U) CFE-DMHA Designation as Disaster Management and Humanitarian Assistance Coordinating Authority for U.S. Pacific Command," October 24, 2013.

U.S. Pacific Command and Center for Excellence in Disaster Management and Humanitarian Assistance, "Memorandum of Understanding Between Commander, United States Pacific Command and Director, Center for Excellence in Disaster Management and Humanitarian Assistance," August 24, 2011.

———, "Memorandum of Understanding Between Commander, United States Pacific Command and Director, Center for Excellence in Disaster Management and Humanitarian Assistance," July 2, 2014.

U.S. Pacific Command Instruction 0530.1, *Command Relationships*, Halawa Heights, Hawaii, December 2014.

U.S. Secretary of Defense, memorandum establishing authority over CFE-DMHA under both PACOM and ASD/SOLIC, April 24, 2000.

Wilcox, Andrew, and Rick Chambers, "Center of Excellence in Disaster Management and Humanitarian Assistance (COE-DMHA): Business Case Analysis," briefing slides, Ford Island, Hawaii: Center for Excellence in Disaster Management and Humanitarian Assistance, undated.